Acknowledgments

Ten years ago, when I started posting the Daily Bailey, I never dreamed it would lead to a book. The fact that it has, I owe to my village of family, friends and Facebook followers who persisted in not only saying I could, but I should publish these stories in the form of a book. Thank you all for pushing me out of my comfort zone and encouraging me to finish this project. I may be the first author to thank Mark Zuckerberg and Facebook for catapulting me to fame as a writer.

There would be no story to tell without Bailey, and I owe this to my daughter Heather. Thank you, Heather, for trusting me enough to love your boy for the rest of his days. Bailey loved you first, and I am certain loved you best until his dying day. You were always the better rider for him, much as I loved him, and I am grateful you did not sell him off for a tidy sum of money when your time with him was done.

Many of the stories Bailey told were inspired by the sage wisdom and patient teachings of my trainer and coach, Chris Scarlett. Thank you, Chris, for taking on this unlikely pair who I'm certain on first appearances was a match made in hell. You took us through our first steps back to competition after he recovered from laminitis, and faithfully walked by our side as many years later, we took our last steps together.

I owe my baby brother Mark Elliot Snyder a debt of gratitude for his technical wizardry in creating our cover. Note to self, when planning to write a book, ensure any photos you will want as a cover have enough pixels or resolution or whatever in God's name is required to be cover worthy. If, like me, you have no idea you're planning to create a book, I will hook you up with my baby brother who works magic. Thank you, Mark, for allowing me to honor Bailey's last request, that the face all his followers came to know, and love is the cover for his book.

Thank you all who have followed our journey on Facebook, this book is for you. It was a privilege to share our stories with you. Bailey's memory lives on in many hearts now, a beautiful and powerful reminder of how story connects us all. Enjoy.

Foreword

I acquired Bailey as a seven or eight-year-old scruffy nondescript bay thoroughbred living out in a field. As most thoroughbreds do, he had a fabulous walk and canter, an atrocious trot, an aversion to rein contact, and was weak in the hindquarters, so had a head bob until he got stronger. I had just come off an amazing Appaloosa that was the definition of a schoolmaster, and truth be told, Bailey wasn't my first choice, but it's what we could afford. We worked together for a while, and he slowly took me up the levels from Beginner Novice to Prelim. He took me to my first FEI event (international event) when I was 16, and we finished 13 out of 52, despite me not owning the proper coat and not knowing nearly enough about Dressage. After realizing he didn't have the scope to go higher, and after a brief stint as a lesson horse, he became Mom's horse, and packed her around Elementary and Beginner Novice, even when she had her eyes closed. At the end of his competition years, he never acquired a single cross-county penalty. He was my go-to horse for everything: I rode him bareback jumping in the sprinklers, read my English homework books on him while doing his conditioning trots before school, used him to drag logs out of the creek so I could jump them, and he babysat the foals when they were weaned. He went with me to school twice, once for farm day, and once to help with my senior project. He was always the boyfriend horse, the lead horse, and the horse you could always pony off of. After I left for Connecticut, I heard Bailey was many a child's first ride, and the horse that taught people how to be around horses. He saw me through high school, my parent's divorce, and two college degrees, as well as my transition from intermediate level rider to professional. He was the first horse that taught me I could train a horse, and that I could teach someone to ride. He was always there when I broke up with a boyfriend or made a big life change, riding and being around him was like slipping on a pair of old fuzzy slippers. When I left for Connecticut Bailey became my mom's anchor, her teammate, confidante, and connection to me. Many nights she spent cleaning his stall, pouring out her love life or work woes to him, and generally after a few hours at the barn with him, came back with a fresh outlook on life and some new answers.

That might not mean much to those non-horse people reading this book, but what it translates to is that Bailey was a rock and a touchstone for me and my mother. Riding or leasing a horse is one thing, but when you own a horse you are responsible for their care 24/7, their medical expenses, their quality of life, their exercise, their health and well-being, and their training and experiences with humans and other horses. That entails spending a considerable part of your life at the barn!

What's special about horses is that they do not speak, and as stewards for the horse, we must learn to read body language and non-verbal cues; it also means they cannot be duplicitous. You learn to interpret their every move, and in turn, understand your own. Having to constantly be on watch for these cues means one truly must slow down, stop multitasking and be mentally present and calm. Combine this with the long hours spent caring for the horse gives one a lot of meditation quality time spent with an honest friend who is an excellent listener.

Over the years both of us have spent so much time around Bailey discussing and ruminating on important decisions that he became like a wise old owl, and it was no surprise when she asked me if she could write something like a blog from his perspective, called the Daily Bailey. As a professional in the industry I have come to learn and appreciate that horses teach you a lot about things not related to horses, and so I thought it was a great idea to share his character with everyone. It was an immediate hit on Facebook, and people coast to coast fell in love with his stories, his anecdotes, and his words of wisdom, even if they hadn't met him!

Tragically, in September of 2018, we lost Bailey to laminitis at the ripe age of 28. His passing has left a huge hole in our lives and many others, and we would like to commemorate him by sharing his wisdom and memories. I know not everyone can own a horse, but hopefully by sharing this more of you can experience the joy and fulfillment that comes with spending so much time with these incredible creatures. I hope you find him as much an inspiration and a guide as I have!

Heather Navarrete
Professional Trainer
Invictus Eventing

To Bailey

You are still the only man I have ever trusted with all my heart

May 7, 2010

The Daily Bailey

"When the world says, 'give up', hope whispers 'Try it one more time" ~ unknown

Life is good today. After two long years and countless trips to Pioneer Equine Hospital to fix my foundered feet, both Rocky the farrier and my vets pronounced me healed. Thank you everyone for all your prayers. After years of going barefoot, I even got shoes! Rocky says most horses who foundered like I did, in all four feet, would have laid down and died from the pain, it would be so bad. He told my Mom I had a great will to live, and it was probably because I loved her so; this made Mom cry, but Rocky was only telling the truth. In the months I have struggled to overcome this, Mom came faithfully and often just sitting in my stall, scratching my ears, and talking to me. Sometimes I would hear her praying, sometimes she would sing to me. She told me I could go home to the light if the pain was too bad, I just had to let her know for sure that's what I wanted. She told me she didn't care if she ever had the chance to sit on my back again, it was enough for her to just be with me, she would love me just the same. We certainly have had a rough go of it, though it is no fault of hers. I'm not the easiest horse to ride and she's not the easiest rider to horse, if you catch my meaning. She'd be much better suited to a drafty thing built like a tank with the patience of a saint than a sensitive thoroughbred like me. But here we are, and we are lucky to have one another. Someone else might have put me down long ago, but she listened with her heart and knew I wasn't ready to go. Love builds bridges where all else fails. We'll sort this thing out and learn to work with one another just like we got through these past two years together – one day at a time.

September 18, 2010

The Daily Bailey

"A horse gallops with its lungs, perseveres with his heart, and wins with his character." ~ Tesio

Life is good today. I took another trip to see Rocky the farrier down at Pioneer, while Mom and the nice lady who drove us enjoyed lots of something called girl talk. I couldn't keep track of much of it, following their conversation was like trying to follow a fart in a windstorm. Whatever, they were happy, I was happy, and it made the day pass faster for all of us. Rocky says there is no more bruising on my sole when he trimmed it, and next time if the x-rays are good, I might even be able to go back to work. I am one lucky horse, that's for sure. Some people still think my Mom is crazy for not giving up long ago, but

I'm thankful she has a passionate heart and a stubborn will. It also doesn't hurt that she has had a soft spot in her heart for me since Heather began riding me all those years ago. How I miss my first girl! Mom says it's a good thing I have an adorable character and a kind eye, otherwise she would have sold me to the Bedouins long ago, whoever they are. I admit, I've engaged in a fair number of shenanigans under saddle, but I've never stopped at a fence and I've never bucked her off, so there's that. Ran backwards at warp speed, spun like a reiner, and bolted like a racehorse, small prices to pay for my dashing good looks and charm. And I have impeccable ground manners, Heather saw to that. Mom told me she loves the way I nicker to her when she comes into the barn – she says it reminds her there's at least one man in the world still happy to see her. She's so funny sometimes! And while I do love her, like any good horse, I fully intend to use this charming character to my advantage as soon as we are back to work.

September 25, 2010

The Daily Bailey

"Bread may feed my body, but a horse feeds my soul." ~ Unknown

Life is good today. My feet feel so much better. I had a good long graze today on some tasty grass, and a nice cool shower when the day was done. Mom says back East the leaves would already be turning colors, and we would be wearing sweaters and drinking hot chocolate. Instead, we continue to swelter in what California calls second summer. I can't repeat what Mom calls it, she's not a fan of our hot dry weather. She had a great ride on Margaux's horse Pilot today, and I think she finally learned the concept of following the horse's mouth with her hands. I'm sorry Pilot had to take one for the team, but if it takes a village to raise one child, I'm sure it takes a nation and an entire barn to raise one good rider. Mom says riding is good for the soul. It's only good for the horse if the rider is any good, which reminds me how lucky I am to have an owner who keeps trying to get good.

February 12, 2011

The Daily Bailey

"Most of the important things in the world have been accomplished by people who kept on trying when there seemed to be no hope at all." ~ Dale Carnegie

Life is good today. A year ago, I was a horse with one foot in the grave, and there was an intervention by those who felt it was time for Mom to put me out of my misery. Today Mom and I had a great lesson – I'm still pretty fly for an old guy. The way Mom carried on you would have thought we did Rolex; I mean it was just some cross-rails, but I don't care. I think we are both thankful we are still kicking it over fences at our respective ages. It has been a very long and painful two years, but I look forward to many more adventures with Mom before we are both turned out to pasture.

July 1, 2011

The Daily Bailey

“The canter is a cure for every evil.” ~ Benjamin Disraeli

Life is good today. I’ve got plenty of good hay, a clean stall and an owner who is a virtual pez dispenser for lovely carrots. She told me last night that a good canter is like vaccine for the soul in a world which seems to have become infected with pessimism. I can’t help but agree, after all, a perfect canter depart is a lovely thing. She always seems to leave the barn with a lighter spirit than she came with, and that us a good thing. I can’t fix the economy, or politics, or the state of our nation because after all, I am just a horse. But I can remind at least one soul that, despite forces which contrive to convince us otherwise, there are still moments of loveliness and joy, and life is still good.

July 28, 2011

The Daily Bailey

“In your mind, you must hold the grandest, most beautiful version of your horse that you can imagine.” ~ unknown

Life is good today. The turnouts have been freshly irrigated, which means new green grass, and I have an owner who thinks I am the grandest and most beautiful thoroughbred on earth. No matter that I am old, a little stiff, cow-hocked, and more than a little stubborn. In her mind, I am a handsome and noble thoroughbred with the heart of a lion, and I love her for this. She works hard every ride to help me resemble that image, not an easy feat by any means. Still she tries, and I love her for that, too. Well that and all the carrots....

August 23, 2011

The Daily Bailey

“I don’t know what organically grown chickens are; I’ve never seen one.” ~Tony Curtis

Life is good today. Turnouts are open again, I’ve got good hay, and the weather is beginning to cool down after this last most dreadful heat wave. If Tony Curtis wants to see organic chickens, he should come to the barn where I live.

I hear we are expecting twenty of them, to produce organic eggs. In fact, a lovely new chicken coop is being built right next to our jump arena, so all the horses can become familiar with our organically feathered friends. I'm unsure how this will all work out – both horses and chickens tend to be a skittish lot. I'll be fine I'm sure, but we are all taking bets on who's horse will be the first to lose their ever-loving mind when a chicken begins flapping about them. Mom thinks it's pretty funny and made one of the boarders laugh by strutting around flapping her elbows and clucking like a chicken – the poor woman nearly rolled off her horse. Mom says it's always a good thing to keep your sense of humor about things which don't make sense, and for a human, she's pretty smart, so I reckon she's right. No sense getting our panties in a bunch, we'll just sit back and wait for the show. I can hardly wait.

September 18, 2011

The Daily Bailey

"Change always comes bearing gifts." ~ Price Prichett

Life is good today. I got to stretch my legs with a good long graze and spend an hour or so with Mom. She told me we need to find a new barn to stay at soon, we've apparently worn out our welcome here, it's time to move on. I suspected this was coming - horses can sense tension, and all the horses have been feeling it lately. I was a little sad at first; Mom says so is she, but sometimes you have to stand up for what you believe in even if it means standing alone. She says at least we are in good company, Val and Hi and Bel got asked to leave as well, so we're not really standing alone after all. I will miss Buckett the most, Mom says so will she, but we will make new friends and have new adventures to write about soon, and she will have peace of mind knowing she can provide all the things I need. She's already looked into other barns in the area, and it doesn't seem to be a problem getting all the bedding I need so I won't get sores on my hocks or my elbows anymore, or the kind of hay I need because I have foundered. That makes us both happy. So, I guess we will be writing some new chapters in our adventures soon. I do hope our new place has lots of green grass to loaf around in!

September 27, 2011

The Daily Bailey " So many tangles in life are ultimately hopeless that we have no appropriate sword other than laughter."~ Gordon Allport

Life is good today. Got to roll around in the turnouts and put back all the dust Mom so carefully washed out of my coat a couple of days ago. Things are falling into place for our new home, and all looks good for us in the future. Mom was drinking a cup of coffee while she tacked me up, and said she will really miss the good footing, until the lady in the next cross-ties over remarked that the footing was worthless if you had to step through a lot of bullshit to use it, which made Mom laugh so hard, coffee came out of her nose. I don't know why they said that, I've never seen any bulls out here, only a couple of jackasses; but it made Mom laugh and that is one of my favorite sounds. She said once that laughter is really God's medicine, and everyone should be taking it. She laughed at being called defiant, too, but that time coffee didn't come out of her nose. She said it was not the worst thing she had ever been called, but probably the truest, and she was proud of it. The true meaning of defiant, she said, is to boldly resist an authority or opposing force; and if everyone was afraid of being called defiant, we might still be a British Colony, the South might still have slaves, and she might still be forced to ride me sidesaddle. Not all authority is reasonable and just, she said, and even Albert Einstein said we shouldn't do anything our conscience tells us not to, even if the state demands it. I don't know who he is, but she says he was a VERY smart man, so I'll take it on faith she's right. She hasn't let me down so far; I know she loves me and will do what's best, so I'm not worried. But I do love to hear her laugh.

November 5, 2011

The Daily Bailey

"Our brightest blazes of gladness are commonly kindled by unexpected sparks." ~ Samuel Johnson

Life is GOOD today. Mom found a wonderful new home for us! They welcomed us into a stall that is so big, you could fit both me AND Beckett in it. And, I have TWO paddocks to choose from! And yes, there is plenty of good green grass for loafing and grazing – the turnouts here are huge! Mom is happy to find we have a tack locker right in the corner of my stall, so now she can keep me company while she sits and cleans tack. I like this idea as well, as it gives me more opportunity to beg carrots. The horse next to me is called Willi; he is very kind, and helped me settle in. Mom and I had a great ride in the covered arena last night, and I'm thinking this will be a very good place for us. It's good to see her happy again. I haven't seen a cat yet, but there are several dogs of varying temper and breeding running about, so chances of a cat surviving here may be slim. I miss Orange Kitty, who would sit in my manger and visit with me at night. Mom says to say thank you, all those who prayed for us into our new safe haven. She says God always works for good for those who love Him and are called according to His purpose. I don't know what that means, but she said to say it, so there you are. I try to do what she says. Well, most of the time.

November 14, 2011

The Daily Bailey "A Sunday well spent brings a week of content." ~ Old Proverb

Life is good today. Mom and I enjoyed a Sunday well spent riding the fence line along the upper pasture in the last light of day. We were pretending to ride the borders of the middle march in the Scottish Lowlands, like her ancestors the Border Reivers. She was playing Scotland the Brave on her phone and told me we were going out on a hot trot to catch a band of raiders who had stolen our cattle, we being of the Armstrong Clan. Oh, what a glorious story she told! Catching a beautiful scarlet sunset, Mom says it doesn't get better than this. I think she's right. What could be better than spending a lovely Sunday afternoon on an adventure with a woman who adores you? Especially when she is carrying a full bag of carrots?

December 5, 2011

The Daily Bailey

"Leadership is the art of getting someone else to do something you want done because he wants to do it." ~ Dwight D. Eisenhower

Life is good today. I've been lounging out in pasture with O'Ryan and Norman, getting fat and sassy on grass and enjoying the December sun. I need this respite after the past few lessons with Mom, which were intense, to say the least. Can I ask who had the bright idea to send her for assertiveness training? I mean, I had a pretty good thing going when I could easily intimidate her by throwing my head up in the air, spinning, backing up at 100 miles an hour, or running sideways like a crab. Oh, don't be shocked, all horses have means of evading work, I'm no different. The fact that I love her doesn't mean I love to work hard. Lately, however, she seems to stick like tick in the saddle, and has, on more than one occasion, tricked me into thinking it was MY idea to drop my head and go forward into a contact. What may I ask is up with that? I'm hoping she doesn't take this leadership thing too far – I'm old enough to know how and still young enough to remember how to throw a few bucks in here and there to remind her who's the boss here.

December 15, 2011

The Daily Bailey "Never judge a work of art by its defects." ~Washington Allston

Life is good today and has been full of surprises. I was the talk of the UC Davis Equine service earlier this week. Nobody could believe what good shape I was in for a nearly nineteen- year old event horse who had foundered in all four feet. And when they saw my x-rays, nobody could believe I could still walk! A very nice vet from Ireland was part of my exam team, and as she was waiting for my new films, she stood with us, and talked to me. She was rubbing her hand over my chest, when her fingers caught that divot in the muscle on the left. Her hand lingered there for a moment, and Mom, noticing this, said she didn't know what it was, but everybody asks her about it, and they say it's a defect of some sort in the muscle. The vet looked up in surprise, and in the most lilting Irish brogue says why it's not a defect at all, it's called a Prophet's Thumb, and legend has in Ireland it's the mark of a great horse! She went on to say that horses with this marking are said to be blessed. And then she slid her thumb right into the groove, to show how it fit perfectly into that little spot. Well, Mom was so delighted to know that the very thing people were calling a defect was actual proof I was indeed a charmed horse. How sweet is that? Mom says that's how it is a lot of the time in life – what we believe to be our imperfections are often our greatest gifts. She said she has never doubted for a moment I was one of the most charmed and lucky thoroughbreds in the universe, surviving all that I'd been through, and she was honored to call me her own.

December 31, 2011

The Daily Bailey

"Year's end is neither an end nor a beginning, it is a going on, with all the wisdom that experience can instill in us." ~ Hal Borland

Life is good today. What an eventful year this has been for us! There have been ugly endings but beautiful beginnings with blessings neither one of us could foresee. There have been new friends, answered prayers, and those petitions we continue to hold before God. Whatever the new year holds for us, Mom says for sure it will be an adventure, and she is very glad I am still along for the ride. Happy New Year everyone!

February 12, 2012

The Daily Bailey

"I don't believe you have to be better than everybody else. I believe you have to be better than you ever thought you could be." ~ Ken Venturi

Life is good today. We had a great weekend schooling the Intro level cross-country course in Fresno! What a motley crew of horse and rider we were. At one time or another, each of our riders were essentially told we were not worth the stall space we took up, give up and move on to another horse. Thank goodness they are all stubborn women, not easily moved by popular opinion. Thanks to their devotion and perseverance and the help of a great trainer, we were able to repay some of the love and care they have poured into us. The fences may have been small, but we showed our riders they were better than they ever thought they could be. We are all looking forward to our next test and clean cross-country rides!

February 24, 2012

The Daily Bailey "Horses do think…not very deeply, perhaps, but enough to get you into a LOT of trouble." ~ P. Johnson ~

Life is good today. I got warm sun and good grass, and a Mom who still loves me, although last night I think she wanted to sell me to a tribe of Bedouins. I thought I was pretty clever, avoiding the outside rein by spinning AND backing up at the same time. She, however, was not amused. To her credit, neither was she unseated – impressive considering she was riding bareback on just a fleece pad. I think she'll forgive me by the time she comes out this afternoon; I'm too adorable for her to stay mad at for long, or so she always tells me. I did overhear her saying something about pushing those buttons when the trainer was around so they could fix them, so I guess I better start thinking about behaving before we need one of those Come to Jesus talks. I've had a few of those with my first girl Heather, and they were not pretty. I think this is where my charming personality needs to keep me out of trouble for the time being.

April 16, 2012

The Daily Bailey

"It's not about being better than someone else; it's about being better than you were yesterday." Kano Jigoro

Life is good today. I had great fun galloping over the cross-country course yesterday! I think I've finally convinced Mom to let me go a little faster. I keep telling her how unfair it is when you own a Ferrari but drive it like a Kia. She reminds me one cannot drive a Ferrari like a Ferrari when one only has the skill set for a Kia, so I will have to be patient. She was very happy with our ribbon, we came in with a respectable placing for our first show back, and she thanked me for all of it. She says it doesn't matter if we take home a ribbon or not, our job isn't just about winning ribbons. Our job is about riding well, every day just a little bit better than we were the day before. We are getting ready to move up a level at the next show, and I'm excited to show her I still remember what Heather taught me. And I still have a fifth gear! LOL. Time to park that Kia for good, baby!

May 1, 2012

The Daily Bailey

“The sweet days of marriage are like heaven on earth; the bad ones strip you of your fear of death.” ~ Sara Ban Breathnach

Life is good today, even though our ride was NOT one of those sweet days of marriage between horse and rider. Mom says I was like fiber today – bound to irritate the crap out of her. I admit, I squirted away from any leg aid she applied, and hollowed my back. She was no less annoying, however, with those bouncing hands and unforgiving elbows. For God’s sake will someone help this woman get steadier hands? It was very nearly one of those ugly fights where, if I had opposable thumbs, we’d be screaming and throwing dishes at one another and scaring the neighbors. Then Mom began to laugh at how stubborn and grumpy we both were, deciding we should simply agree to disagree, and go for a nice walk. I’m glad she saw it my way, as it put us BOTH in a better mood.

May 6, 2012

The Daily Bailey

"Nothing in life is to be feared, it is only to be understood. Now is the time to understand more, that we may fear less." ~ Marie Curie

Life is good today. Mom and I are hanging out in the pasture, planning our next adventure at Woodside Spring Horse Trials! Now we had an AWFUL experience there, some years back, and it's been her personal boogeyman ever since. Nothing seriously hurt but our confidence, but in this sport, confidence means everything, especially when you are galloping at a fence that puts skid marks on your shorts. Yesterday, we went back to school that course, because Mom says you can't let fear define you or your world will simply become small. And you know what? This time, it was different. Thanks to Chris, we stared that boogeyman right in the eye and said: WATCH THIS! Because now she understands fences ask questions, and now she understands how to approach and set up for the fence, so she knows the right answer.

So now, when her eyes are telling her HOLY CRAP that's a scary looking fence! She can say yes, it is, and this is how we ride it. Woohoo! We had a blast going over the roll tops, some coops, we even did a half-coffin! (Why would they name a jump after something that holds dead people?) With each jump, the boogeyman got smaller and Mom's smile got bigger. Bertrand Russell once said the experience of overcoming fear is extraordinarily delightful, and by the look on her face, I would have to agree.

May 13, 2012

The Daily Bailey "Brave hearts do not back down." ~Sophocles

Life is good today. We didn't get to jump today, because my foot is still sore, but I was glad to hang out with Mom while she took care of it. I like it when she talks to me, and I could tell today she needed to talk. She asked me if I remembered Patrick, the little boy who rode me one summer, the one who clung to my neck like a tick when I suddenly broke into a canter in the round pen. Well how could I forget? He was not more than six or seven, but never flinched when Mom shouted to him "Hang on!" and that he did 'til I slowly came down to a walk. She said

Patrick is all grown up and became a Marine. Yesterday, he got orders to deploy to Afghanistan. She had to explain what deployment was, and I still have no idea where or what Afghanistan is, but when she told me there was no grass there, only desert, that was all I needed to know. I told her I wouldn't like it there at all. Mom says neither will Patrick, but those are his orders and he must go. I know he will be a brave soldier; look how brave he was riding me! That boy has some good nerve. Still, I see the worry in Mom's eyes, after all he is her godson. She began talking to God about him; I know many people think animals cannot talk to God, but of course we do; after all, He made us! I rested my head on Mom's shoulder and told her don't worry, we can BOTH talk to God and ask Him to please bring Patrick home again safe and sound. I think she liked that.

June 3, 2012

The Daily Bailey "Patience is the ability to idle your motor when you feel like stripping your gears." ~ Barbara Johnson

Life is good today. Mom says I get to hang out and be a pasture ornament for a bit until my feet grow a little. She wants to strangle the farrier -, we were on such a good run and looking forward to Woodside. I'm just one of four horses that went lame after shoeing, so we're in good company but that is no consolation. I'm fine with it, but she's pulling her hair out. She says we'll just work on refining our aids and keeping me flexible until we can train again. She had the chiropractor come out and adjust me – aaahhh that felt good. Mom says I have a new sister out in Connecticut, named Mattie, who belongs to my first girl, Heather. I hope I get to meet Mattie one day – she better be good for Heather; I love that girl and miss her so much. Mom says she might go back to Connecticut to visit and bring me back a brother, some huge horse named Booker. I'm not sure I like the idea of sharing Mom, but it might be fun to have a big brother if he likes his withers scratched.

July 4, 2012

The Daily Bailey

"While we are mourning the loss of our friend, others are rejoicing to meet him behind the veil." ~John Taylor

Life is good today. My dear old friend Beckett stopped by today, on his way to the Light. He couldn't stay long, as they were waiting for him on the other side – but he insisted he could not leave without coming to bid me farewell. We've shared many adventures, and I've missed him a great deal, so I was delighted to see him again. We laughed about the time we went to Ram Tap for my show, and he swore there were pink flying monkeys lurking in every tree down by the river. We swear our moms never laughed so much. We talked about the many trail rides we enjoyed, helping our moms solve all the world's problems, if only for a day. It was a lovely visit. Beckett told me Chappie, Bonito and Star are on the other side, and that as far as the eye could see, there was nothing but the most tender green grass. And no stalls! We can wander wherever we like! Sharon's Dad is there, and Fiona's mom, even my Mom's mom – he says the place is full of people waiting to welcome us. He said to tell my Mom he remembers his promise to her, and to thank her for all the little acts of kindness. He also said not to let her not to cry too much about not being there to pray him into the Light.

(He snorts and laughs, reminding me Sharon calls this Mom's version of last rites.) Beckett says animals are closer to the angels than we know, and whether Mom prayed him across or not, it wasn't like God didn't see him coming. Still, he says, tell her thank you. I make Beckett promise not to visit her in his spirit body, because it will totally unravel her, and remind him to visit her in her dreams, she would like that. Beckett gives me one last scratch on the withers, and I hang my head over his for one last minute. As he turns and trots away, I am thankful he came to say goodbye. I rejoice that his soul is now free from an aged, broken body and he can gallop through endless green hills until we meet again. And I watch as he slowly disappears into the Light.

August 16, 2012

The Daily Bailey

"Even if happiness forgets you a little bit, never completely forget about it." ~Jacques Prevert

Life is good today. The heat is not as fierce as it has been, and the grass in our turnouts is tasty and green. Brighton and I are having great fun snatching each other's fly masks off, much to the frustration of our moms, but it's one of those games' horses play to pass the time until our moms come to visit. Mom told me today that her sister Wendy passed into the Light a few days ago, just like Beckett. I already knew she was very sad; horses know these things before humans speak a word. That's why Brighton, Pepe, Armand, and even the mares came to the front of their stalls and nickered to her as she walked down the barb aisle. They know she doesn't give carrots until she leaves, so this was their way of telling her they were present for her in her sorrow. We went for a nice hack, into the field across the street where we watched the sun set while she had a long talk with God and her sister as we walked around the field. I felt her sorrow deeply. I began to worry this loss would make her forget all the goodness and happiness her own life has and has yet to offer. Some of you don't believe God speaks through a horse but I'm telling you, that's exactly what He did. Right then and there

I reminded her how sweet my face is hanging over the stall door to greet her; I made her remember all my silly moments that made her laugh, how good our jump lesson was last Sunday, and how I taught her she could fly on the cross-country course. She patted my neck and told me I was her once-in-a-lifetime horse, who saved not only her faith but her sanity on more than one occasion. And, thank you very much, her butt over more than a few fences. When I heard her laugh at that remark, I knew she would be all right, because she was remembering the grace and humor still very much alive in her life. Bailey, she said, we are going to squeeze every drop of joy from this life we can, because it's the only thing we can take with us when we go. In fact, if the only way to have a life is to commit to it like crazy, then game on, we're jacking up those fences to 2 foot 9 inches for our next jump school. Yes ma'am, I think she'll be just fine.

August 28, 2012

The Daily Bailey

"There's nothing greater in the world than when somebody on the team does something good, and everybody gathers around to pat him on the back. ~" Billy Martin

Life is good today. Resting up from the schooling at Twin Rivers over the past weekend – everyone did so well! Keen Eddie lived up to his name, taking Tara over the Preliminary course like it was Intro; Coquetta was ALL fired up (boy she sure is a pretty chestnut mare) with Aimee, who looked like she was having way too much fun; Tasha and Sarge were definitely in charge going into the training level water complex and out over the coop; Hunch was a cross-country machine taking Sharon out over the Training level Trakhener – she was smiling so wide she probably had bugs in her teeth. Goose was my favorite, because he literally piaffed up to the down bank like it was part of a freestyle. What a character! Bel did her first big girl cross-country jumps, so it won't be long before we will have to stop calling her Green Bean. I felt my way over a few jumps, which rattled Mom a bit, but she did a good job holding it together all things considered. And we got to cross one more boogeyman off our list by schooling here! I didn't get to see Emma's or Stephanie's horse, but I hear one of them will be practicing some jumps in a straight line.

Our moms left US all at the barn while they went out to the Basque restaurant, which was totally unfair as why should we not have sangria? We did most of the heavy lifting, as Chris would say. But they were all in such a good mood the next day, it didn't matter. Mom says it wasn't the sangria that made everyone happy, it was all the encouragement you get from spending time with good horsewomen who share a common goal. For the most part, eventing is a solitary sport – the hours of training and practice we spend in the arena after work or on weekends are often spent alone. Getting together and celebrating everyone's progress, no matter how small, is just the fuel we need sometimes to keep us showing up at the barn day after day when everyone else is heading home to change into sweats and watch HGTV. And here I thought seeing that adorable white snip on my thoroughbred face was reason enough to keep her come out to the barn every night! I suppose I can forgive her that, she seldom misses a night. Still….

September 15, 2012

The Daily Bailey

"At its finest horse and rider are not joined by tack but by trust each one reliant upon the other, each one the selfless guardian of the other's very well being." ~ Unknown

Life is good today. Mom is in seventh heaven after our jump lesson today. She finally found my accelerator button, and for once was not afraid to USE it. Ah, feels good to be driven like the Ferrari I am! We had some lovely jumps. She said they broke the mold when they made me, and that I'm the only man she's ever trusted. (which is probably the God's honest truth) That made me laugh. Of course she can trust me! How else would I show you how much I appreciate your love and care? Now stop being so silly and open that bag of carrots, and nobody gets hurt.

October 8, 2012

The Daily Bailey

"Praise the bridge that carried you over." ~ George Colman

Life is good today. I am glad the heat is gone for now, but my fuzzy coat is already growing in, which makes for a sweaty horse after practice. We have one last show we are working on, then Mom says I can retire and take it easy. I'm not sure I like the idea of having no job, but I tell you one thing I will not miss a minute of and that is dressage! At first, I worried she might send me away to a retirement home, but she assures me I'll be with her forever. She says I've more than earned that for all I've done for her and Heather – I carried t! hem far beyond what they thought possible. I miss Heather! I heard she took first place on her new horse Mattie – I'm so proud of her. Mom says Heather has lots of new students, and they all seem to be doing well under her coaching. I wish I could meet them one day and tell them stories about Heather and what we did on the cross-country courses. I hope Heather comes to visit me in my retirement, and that she brings a LOT of carrots.

October 14, 2012

The Daily Bailey

"The truth is incontrovertible; malice may attack it, ignorance may deride it, but in the end, there it is." ~ Winston Churchill

Life is good today, at least for me. Not all horses are this lucky, trust me. Some are suffering even as we speak at the hands of those who put profit above good horse management and common human decency, all the while trying to convince you this is the only way to run a successful business. As my granny would say, these people have more nerve than a bad tooth. If I had my way, I'd make some sort of identifying mark appear on their forehead, so the unsuspecting people who send them their children to train or their horses to board would know at once the kind of beast they are dealing with. Like lepers, I would force them to exist on the margins of society dependent upon the mercy of tenderhearted souls like those who weep with compassion for the horses who suffered under their care for greed, and for the innocents who suffered out of ignorance, not knowing there was a better way. Yes sir, that is what I would call justice. I am very lucky because I have had NONE of these awful people in my life. My mother would sooner starve than see me go hungry or cold, and especially not my first girl

Heather who I love with all my heart. I am glad they are both fierce women, who are not afraid to stand up for those who have no voice. I am glad they are relentless, speaking the truth for those of us who have no voice, even though it costs them dearly at times. Peace of mind is priceless. Keep speaking the truth for our sake!

November 6, 2012

The Daily Bailey

"Everyone is the age of their heart." ~ Guatemalan proverb

Life is good today. It is election day, and thankfully I cannot vote as I have no opposable thumbs – but if I did, I would vote for whoever stops all the good hay from being sold to China, I can tell you that much. I had a great time with Mom this past weekend at the Event Derby – for an old guy, I showed her I still had plenty of go! Neither one of us is a spring chicken, to be honest, but we showed the younger ones we still got game. In our hearts, we don't measure our age in years, and that suits both of us. As long as Mom's game, I'm going to give her everything I've got, because she thinks I'm the grandest and most adorable thoroughbred ever. I am, of course, but I try not to let it go to my head.

November 13, 2012

The Daily Bailey

"If you are losing a tug of war with a tiger, give him the rope before he gets to your arm; you can always buy a new rope." ~ Max Gunther

Life is good today, even though the week got off to a rocky start. I can't help it, sometimes Mom is so stiff and unforgiving with her hands and it sends me over the edge. I just was not in the mood for flat work AGAIN. I tried putting my head straight up in the air and hollowed my back, which was a mistake because it only made her pull on my mouth more. When that didn't work, I spun around and backed up down the entire arena at about a hundred and fifty miles an hour, and when that didn't work, I tried crashing us into the wall, and when that didn't work I simply would not move forward at all. By this time, I know she's crying, I know she's scared, but neither one of us wants to give up the fight. She's afraid I'm going to rear straight up in the air and fall over on her. I'm afraid she will continue trying to put me back on the bit, and we will NEVER get to the end of this lesson. Finally, I back us into a corner of the arena, and by now we are both frantic. Chris is standing in the middle of the arena, sizing up the situation, and tells Mom 'just stop. Let him stand there for a few minutes.' Mom's shaking, I'm shaking, but she 'gives me the rope' and trusts her trainer to be right. Within seconds, the fight is over as quickly as it began. Now nobody loses an arm and we both live to ride another day. After a few minutes, Mom cues me to walk on, and I do, straight toward Chris, who thank God is the calm voice of reason in all of this. She says Mom won the discussion, but I am not so sure, I think we just agreed to disagree. That's how riding is some days, you never want to win the battle and lose the war. Fortunately, we both have forgiving natures and hold no grudges, at least toward one another. She's far too kind to stay mad for long. She reminds me I have plenty of other endearing qualities that make the occasional battle tolerable, if not pleasant. Mom says half the battle is knowing when to fight anyway, and today was just not the day. I think I'm pretty lucky to have such a good Mom and a wise, patient trainer, don't you?

December 18, 2012

The Daily Bailey

"We cannot cure the world of sorrow, but we can choose to live in joy." ~ Joseph Campbell

Life is good today. My old friend Hi (and I do mean old, because at 27 he is the equivalent age of an 80-year-old man) has surprised us all. After clinging to the edge of death for days after surgery for a strangulated lipoma, he made a miraculous recovery literally hours before the end of his suffering was planned to happen. Talk about an 11th hour rescue! I guess he figured there was still hope for him, and if there was hope there was a purpose, and if he had a purpose on this earth, well he just better be about it. Mom calls Hi Val's best man, seeing as he is the only man who has stuck with her throughout the roller coaster of her life for the past 27 years. Mom's glad Val didn't have to say goodbye just yet; we all need some hope to cling to right now, after all the tragedy we've seen with the shooting in Sandy Hook. She will take the moment, however small, to help remind us life still holds some inherent goodness. Twenty children shot and killed in their classrooms at an elementary school. I have no words. I am only a horse, but I would send moments of hope and healing to all those grieving this terrible loss, if I could. Mom says the most powerful thing we can do right now is pray that they will be reassured knowing God walks with them, even in the midst of their deepest sorrow. And then we do just that, while she stands with me while I graze in the field.

December 24, 2012

The Daily Bailey

"The angels are always near to those who are grieving, to whisper to them that their loved ones are safe in the hand of God." ~The Angels Little Instruction Book

Life is good today. Mom came to take me for a walk and let me stretch my legs to graze in the back field. The rain keeps us cooped up, but it sure makes the grass tasty. Mom and I shared a good laugh when she told me half the world was disappointed and half was relieved that the Mayan calendar did not in fact, predict the end of the world, and we are all still here. Well at least most of us, she said. She's missing her sister, and her Mom, and those who have passed on before. She knows many of her friends are missing loved ones, and she's a little sad for them, too. Her heart is just breaking thinking about the parents from Sandy Hook who are grieving right now. Mom's glad both her children are home for Christmas this year, and so am I. I was so happy my girl Heather came for a visit. It was a such a treat to see her – sometimes right before I fall asleep, I think about the adventures we had; I'm so blessed to have been her horse. Mom hands out carrots to all the horses, wishing each of them a Merry Christmas: Inca, Weber, May, Pepi, Maverick, and that other hooligan who is Mia's horse. Mom told me I was one of her best Christmas blessings, and told me about how Christmas started in a stable all those years ago. She says it seems fitting, she supposes, to be celebrating Christmas Eve in a barn instead of a church, though she likes church well enough. She gives me one last kiss on the nose, walks down the aisle and turns out the light. Merry Christmas to all, and God bless us everyone.

December 31, 2012

The Daily Bailey

"But friendship is precious, not only in the shade, but in the sunshine of life, and thanks to a benevolent arrangement the greater part of life is sunshine." ~ Thomas Jefferson

Life is good today. I took Mom for a spin down the driveway this afternoon, and I do mean spin. She was all reins at the buckle, and we were enjoying the sun, when a horse-eating monster darted out from that big bush at the end of the driveway, I mean how was I to know the bush was haunted? I did a 180 and thank God Mom's balance has improved (thanks to equestrian boot camp) because she just rolled with it, and then started laughing. She tried to tell me it was a rabbit, but even so, hasn't she ever seen Night of the Lepus??? Giant rabbits took over a town in Texas! Maybe she thinks it can't happen here, I don't know, but I'm not taking any chances. She said it was such a good spin, I would give any cutting horse a run for his money. I hope she's not getting any bright ideas here. Have you seen the size of those western saddles? Mom says the year is over tonight, and I am her New Year's Eve date; that means we've been here at our new barn a year! We are both so happy here - Mom says the only thing that would make it happier is if Luke Bryan started cleaning stalls and they installed an espresso bar in that cute little shed down by the dressage court. And what a year it has been! We have both lost old friends and dear family because they have gone to the light before us, but we've also made new friends. Babies will be born in the coming year, marriages celebrated, and we take comfort in that while we mourn for those no longer here. Boogeymen have been laid to rest as we faced old fears, and new challenges are on the horizon. Mom says the country needs a big ole boss mare to show those hooligans in Washington how a herd needs to be run, and that made me laugh because I know she is right. I remember how Jungle Lace went 50 shades of crazy on Stone that day he jumped into the pasture and threatened her foal. She was all teeth bared, ears pinned back, and he got more than one taste of the business end of her hind feet. But he came to an agreement right quick. Mom says she doesn't know if there will be much agreement in Washington tonight, but as we watched the sun go down on this last day of the year, she says whatever comes me, we'll ride it out together with God, like always. Happy New Year everybody!

January 15, 2013

The Dailey Bailey

"You can't teach feel, you have to experience it." ~ Bill Dorrance

Life is good today. Mom usually gives me Tuesdays off, but I didn't want to work anyway – it's too cold. Mom laughs and tells me I'm a weenie, because she grew up in Appalachia, or so she says. When I have to wait for a school bus in four feet of snow with a temperature of 6 below zero, then she says I can complain. But I was born here, so I tell her it FEELS like 6 below zero when you clip me naked and I must go out in temperatures hovering around thirty degrees. It's all about the feel, I tell her, with a snarky little smile. We've been working a lot on feel these days, because riding is a lot like dancing. You're supposed to feel your partner's moves and follow them. Mom, she's not too good about the following thing, so I bet she's hard to dance with, too. She tries really hard, so I try to be patient with her. Imagine how you might feel if you had a metal bar in your mouth, and one moment someone yanks the bar into your back teeth, and the next moment shoves you forward into it from behind; it's not a pretty picture. Now suppose you had to carry that person on your back, and every time you turned your body this way or that to stay balanced, the person on top got off balance and then got tense and stiff. And instead of holding each other's hand, which is what contact on the bit is supposed to feel like, you are locked in the equestrian version of Mortal Kombat. Welcome to my world, men. But thank God, if I have the Helen Keller of riders, we have the Annie Sullivan of trainers. Chris Scarlett ranks right up there with Mother Theresa and Gandhi, if you ask me. Like how many times has she reminded Mom a loose rein is not necessarily a kind rein, relax and let your leg get long? And then, in our lesson last Sunday, I don't know how it happened, but she finally GOT it. Chris told her to just allow ME to move the reins, and because Mom's balance has improved, she was able to relax her seat, lower her back and just absorb my forward motion without pulling on me or against me. Wow that felt good – and I went nice and forward and ROUND, which is the Holy Grail of dressage. I don't know who was happier, Mom or Chris, but I was happiest – after all I'm the one with the bar in my mouth carrying someone on my back. Now that she begins to learn the language of cooperation, my job becomes easier and far more pleasurable. I am glad for the rest today, while she is at work tending the walking wounded and the worried well; we worked hard. Next lesson, Chris says we'll work on that same feel in both directions, so whatever happened, I'm hoping it sticks.

January 21, 2013

The Daily Bailey

"The way of progress is neither swift nor easy." ~ Marie Curie

Life is good today. Mom has become a woman possessed. After years of searching for the Holy Grail of riding, the one key principle which allows her to unlock the secrets of the equitational universe, she realized it is all about the seat. This discovery transformed her into a woman on a mission, determined to learn everything she can so she can acquire this thing called seat. She's been reading books on Classical Dressage, and I swear I heard her trying to channel someone named Antoine de Pluvinel, and Nuno Oliveira, who she said were masters of the art of classical dressage. All I can say is, it's a good thing the Long Island Medium doesn't come to the barns – we don't need any more encouragement to invite spirit. This is not the funniest part. Mom practices walking around on me without stirrups or reins, trying to lift her thighs away from the saddle in the most unflattering position, if you ask me. She says the last time she held that position for any length of time, she ended up delivering a baby, and her life was very different after that. I certainly hope that does not happen this time – the last thing we need is another little body flopping around up there with her – one is quite enough, thank you. Progress is painstaking, as she can only hold the position for a few strides, but she asks me to be patient, Rome wasn't built in a day. Apparently, this exercise helps her develop what is called a three-point seat, allowing her to move with my back instead of bouncing on it or bracing against it. Or worse, bouncing and bracing while balancing on my mouth with the reins, so I'm all for anything that helps prevent that, no matter how ridiculous it looks. And bit by tiny bit, I think it IS getting better. We did have a great lesson today; Chris gave Mom some exercises to practice, which help Mom learn to ride me more correctly. In my case, this involves whatever chicanery Mom can engage in while tricking me into believing it was my idea to go correctly all along. I suppose if this keeps her happy and me sound, it's all good, but trickery none the less. Mom worked harder than I did for a change, I think she needs some fitness training. After our lesson, she put me out in the pasture with Pepi for a nice long graze. Not a bad way at all to spend a Sunday, if you ask a horse.

February 2, 2013

The Daily Bailey

"The older you get, the more important it is not to act your age." ~ Ashleigh Brilliant

Life is good today. I got to say hello to the vet that saved my life a few years ago. He was quite surprised to see how good I look, considering my age and all I'd been through. Mom and I finally got to do some jumping today, and it's about time. This flat work thing is about to drive me crazy. If I had to go in one more circle…. We started out small, at 2 feet, but we had a great time. Jumping is my favorite thing. Do you know that I have not one refusal on my show record? Nope, not a one. I would have jumped the moon for Heather if she asked – love that girl with all my heart. Now, I'm trying to teach her mother to sit chilly in the saddle, as Chris says, and not get ahead of me in case I need to put an extra stride in. Mom is finally starting to feel what lead we are on after the fence, glad that light bulb is finally going on. I can't fault her; she is getting better but we've a long way still to go. For a 19-year-old horse, I still have much to teach her – we're both happy she hasn't put me out to pasture yet. She says I'm stuck with her because she's too old for a paper route, too young for social security, and too tired for an affair.

March 4, 2013

The Daily Bailey

"In life, a person will come and go from many homes. We may leave a house, a town, a room, but that does not mean that those places leave us. Once entered, we never entirely depart the homes we make for ourselves in the world. They follow us, like shadows." ~ Ari Berk ~

Life is good today. The orchards are all in bloom, and the sun has been nice and warm with my old and aching joints. Mom was here today and told me she finally decided she had enough of this brutal commute and was putting the house up for sale. She wants to be closer to me, and my new potential brother or sister, and closer to work. Spending two or more hours commuting is wearing on her patience and her back. She's sad to leave the neighborhood and the home where she raised Heather and her brother Ryan, but now that they're grown and living on their own, she'd just as soon be closer to me and the barn. I'd like that, too. If we had our wishes, I'd live right on a property with her, wandering about at will, but she says that's not in the cards yet. We had a great lesson today, working on our cues and lightness in the bridle. Chris showed her how forward and light I could be using the most subtle of cues. Now when they made my Mom, they left out the button one pushes when one wants subtle, so the learning curve was steep but I'm very glad Chris is teaching her. Mom's a work in progress, for sure, but I am patient because I know she loves me and because she has a seemingly endless supply of carrots. I hope one day she finds a place for us with room for me, so I can wander around and poke my head in the window and scare the bejeesus out of her one morning as she sits drinking her morning coffee. Oh, I am a wicked little pony for thinking that, but it certainly would be a sight to behold.

March 30, 2013

The Daily Bailey

"It is the best of lessons if the horse gets a season of repose whenever he behaves to his rider's satisfaction." ~Xenophon

Life is good today. Spring weather has finally arrived, and it's a good thing. My old bones don't handle winter as well as they used to. Coquetta sent us a letter from Switzerland, where she moved with Aimee, and says it's very cold in the barn where she now lives. I miss her, but I'm glad I'm staying right here. Mom gives me more days off now, because I am semi-retired. She doesn't want to wear my parts out too soon, as she wants us to have many more trail rides with me in the years ahead. Don't tell Chris, but I am not missing dressage one bit. I don't mind jumping small fences now and then – jumping has always been my favorite part of eventing. Mom told me she's looking at a couple of horses this weekend and might be bringing back a brother or sister for me. I hope it's a sister because I like girls. She also told me she's going to be living right here with me in the apartment over the barn for the next few months, so we can have coffee together every morning if I like. I can't wait! She is selling her house to move closer to me, the barn and her job. She must really love me a lot if she is willing to do that. She said I've earned a good rest for all I've done for her and for Heather, but all I've really done is love them back the only way a good horse knows how. I understand how hard it is for Mom to think about riding any other horse but me – we know each other's every mood, and by now we are as comfortable with one another as an old pair of slippers. I know it makes her sad to move onto another horse, but we both know I can't give her enough saddle time as she needs right now to keep progressing. So, I try to reassure her, and remind her that as long as we are still together, life is good, I am happy, and it will be all right.

March 31, 2013

The Daily Bailey

"No road is long with good company." ~Turkish proverb

Life is good today. So, it looks as if I'll be getting a brother after all. Mom says the mare was quite fancy, but she was way more forward than Mom was comfortable with. I don't know why she doesn't appreciate fast horses – Aunt Faith says she drives like she subs for Jeff Gordon at NASCAR. In the end, the little quarter horse who has been there and done it all felt just right. Mom says he isn't fancy, but he's a good boy and will take great care of her, and that's exactly how I would want it. I'm not fancy by any means, but I'm a good boy, and I always do my best. I can't wait to meet him – Mom says his name is Mr. C, which stands for Cogburn. Chris says it's an alphabetical progression, because they both call me Mr. B sometimes. Mom says he's littler than me, so I must make sure Pepi doesn't pick on him in turnout; big brothers are supposed to do that sort of thing. Mom also says he's quite fat, as he's been living out in pasture, but really, has she seen the size of her own butt lately? It will be good for both of them to work out more and eat less. Right now, she's working on the paperwork with his owners, but will let me know when he's coming so I can meet him. I'm ever so glad Chris found her a good and safe horse to pick up where we had to leave off. As long as he remembers I was here first, I'm sure we'll get along just fine

April 25, 2013

The Daily Bailey

"A barn is a sanctuary in an unsettled world, a sheltered place where life's true priorities are clear." ~ Lauren Davis Barker

Life is good today. Mom has literally moved in with me. well, not into my stall, exactly, but into the little apartment here. She can see me from her upstairs bedroom window! In fact, that's how she saw that one of the mares got loose the other night- she looked out to see what the ruckus was, and there was some big old chestnut mare, flirting with Weber! Well here comes Mom, in her nightshirt, jeans and paddock boots, hair all cattywampus, glasses half-cocked on her nose, to halter the little trollop and put her back to bed. My what a sight, don't think I've ever seen her look like that! I really like it when she drinks her morning coffee with me.

She says she'll bring the kitties out to meet me once they settle down a bit, I'm happy to have cats again because I miss the orange kitty from my old barn. He used to come and hang out on my water bucket and talk to me. She also told me that we get a puppy soon, which I am also excited about - as jealous as I was of that old dog Buck, I must admit I miss him, too. The last two nights we've had a beautiful full moon for our night rides. Mom says the sale of the house is enough to drive her to drink, it is not turning out to be as easy as she thought. But, she says, she only questions her sanity until she sits in the saddle and we take those first few steps. It's then she realizes she is home, doing what's most important to her right now. Humans have such a complex way of thinking about things - horses can only be in the moment, so it's hard for me to understand all the emotions that make her decisions difficult. But I'm glad that when she's in that moment with me, it all becomes clear.

June 16, 2013

The Daily Bailey

"Fear is sometimes an inexplicable panic, and sometimes a justified reaction." ~ Unknown

Life is good today, but I think Mom has had enough of rural country living. Her house has sold, but since she hasn't found the right one to buy yet, she's still living in the apartment over the barn. She loves being able to look out her bedroom window and see right into my stall but Living in a barn surrounded by open fields with the attendant wildlife does have its drawbacks. Have you ever seen a human being vibrate? They say a horse only has a brain the size of a walnut but let me tell you if a horse walks by and sees a four-foot snake in the wash rack, you can bet he isn't going to be running in place howling like a banshee. I think the only thing holding Mom back was the fact that Mr. C was on the end of the lead rope she was holding and would not let go of. Built like a small army tank, the sheer weight of him stopped her like an anchor when she got to the end of that rope, and there she was, vibrating and screaming until Brandon came and took the snake away. I can't even repeat what Mom told Brandon she would do if he let that snake go anywhere near the barn again. The next thing I know, she's on her cell to the realtor, and this is what I heard: "NOW. I want a house

NOW. I am tired of having to hike out to the northwest corner of the pasture and put foil on my head to get a cell signal, slow speed internet, and fending off wildlife. I am not Steve Irwin for God's sake and look what happened to him. Get in your Lexus SUV, pick me up, and by God we are buying a house TODAY. "

July 15, 2013

The Daily Bailey "Grief is the price we pay for love." ~ Elizabeth II

Life is good today. Another old friend has just passed over into the Light My good friend Hi, who splashed with me in Lagoon Valley just one year ago to celebrate his 28th birthday, has crossed over. He has had a rough go of it this past year, what with intestinal surgery, followed by several months of complications, but oh how much more life did he enjoy in the seven months following that. He celebrated one more birthday with a splash in the lake, took Val's daughter Syd to her very first horse show, and received endless hugs and kissed from all who loved him, including Mom. After his surgery, it was in fact, all he seemed to want – the feeling of someone's arms wrapped around that great head of his in a wonderful hug. Mom will always remember what a kind, bright eye he had, with a twinkle that made you feel he was delighted to see you. He was the only horse she ever allowed to nuzzle her backside while she was bent over blanketing him. She knew he had no teeth to bite her with, having lost them some time ago. I know his people are sad, as I am too. The reality of getting older is that you begin to say goodbye to many of your cherished companions. It can be a bit lonely, being left. I do hope Hi looks up Beckett when he gets to the Light, but most of all I hope he gets his teeth back, so he can graze again on fresh green grass. Beckett says there are pastures there as far as the eye can see. Maybe he will meet his grandfather Secretariat there! I hope people get to read the story Mom wrote for him, about being Val's best man, because he was, you know. Hi was the love in her life that was solid as an anchor. Mom says horses are like that for some of us; they ground us, keep us sane, and remind us we are deeply loved. Godspeed my good friend Hi. Know you were very much loved and will be dearly missed.

September 18, 2013

The Daily Bailey

"Those who were seen dancing were thought quite mad by those who could not hear the music." ~ Friedrich Nietszsche

Life is good today. But could someone explain to me what it is about Spanish guitar music which inspires a woman to do things that, in her right mind, she never would consider? Is it not enough that she tempts fate by stubbornly refusing to give up eventing for more sedentary pursuits? Must she try the patience of saints like me, by dabbling in the art of the Spanish Vaqueros? Here we are, having a nice ride around the arena, when she picks up the six foot long lunge whip and announces to me that we are going to practice dragging it alongside us so she can see what it would be like to ride with a garrocha. I have no idea what that is, but it sounds like it itches. so, my eyeballs pop out of my head, but ok, we're dragging it alongside us and I'm good with that. I'm beginning to wonder if Chris, her trainer, knows the woman has taken leave of her senses. Then, then, she plants that lunge whip like the US flag in a lunar landing SMACK! and I'm supposed to walk a circle around it. And after that, canter a circle around it! At our age, neither one of us is that balanced in the canter (or the mind, I'm beginning to think) but by the grin on her face SHE was obviously enjoying herself. Oh, the things I do for love. And love me she does. Once she was satisfied we had given it a good try, she put the lunge whip down, and wrapped her arms around my neck, and told me how much she loved me, and how thankful she was she got to at least try it first with me, because she feels safest on me. She told me don't worry, she would never make me her Doma Vaquera horse, she knows it's not my cup of tea. That was a relief! But what delighted me most was, even in my semi-retirement, I still have something to offer her for all she has given me. Yes, life is very, very good today.

November 16, 2013

The Daily Bailey

“Life gives us brief moments with another…but sometimes in those brief moments we get memories that last a lifetime.” ~ Unknown

Life is good today. The nights are turning colder, and my winter coat has been coming in; as she was brushing me last night, Mom said I looked far more like a yak than the thoroughbred she knows me to be. She hopes I appreciate being able to winter over without a clipping this year. Now that I am retired, there’s no need for clipping as my hardest work will be walking around the property, unless I feel otherwise inclined. I’m not sure how I feel about this retirement thing – it’s a mixed bag if you ask me. I know she is working with that fat little sorrel they are turning out with me, and while my joints are thankful for the rest, at times I miss my job and wish for just a moment to be working again. Mom must have been thinking the same thing, because as she curried and brushed, she laughed as she remembered some of our adventures together. Bailey, she said, you have given me some of the most incredible moments of my life. Remember how we flew over that turkey feeder in Fresno we called the Green Booger? What a show that was! Our first time together on a cross-country course, and my first show in nearly ten years. And remember those big green roll tops at Ram Tap? Lord I almost pooped my pants, but you hopped over them like cross-rails; you didn't miss a beat. And the time I lost my stirrups in a jump lesson over the oxer, and I landed sideways, clinging to your neck like an Indian shooting arrows at buffalo? You taught me to fly, Bailey, and I will never, never forget that. And she wrapped her arms around my neck and we just stood there for several minutes, grateful for each other and the journey we have shared. We have certainly had some adventures. I am glad to know that while retired from work, I have not retired in her heart.

January 8, 2014

The Daily Bailey

"You always think you could have done more. That's why you need a friend — to tell you that you did all you could." ~ Robert Brault

Life is good today. Although the turnouts are closed for watering, at least the weather has warmed, and we are not up to our tail docks in snow as those stabled on the East coast. Mom said if I was feeling good enough to try to buck Miss Heather off on our little trail ride, I was feeling good enough to be her spare horse now that the other one is laid up with a sore foot. I told her the sturdiness of quarter horses has been highly overestimated these days but who listens to a horse? especially a thoroughbred - known for their delicate constitution and high-strung nature! It was just her and me in the indoor covered - winter riding is like that - only the determined ride in the cold and dark. I couldn't help but smile when she settled into that Devocoux and we started off at a walk - a nice, forward, thoroughbred walk I might add, and I could feel her whole body just relax and fall into that old rhythm we once had together. I also couldn't help but notice her elbows have become far more forgiving, her contact steadier, and her balance better. She's also got more control over that upper body than she used to, I'll say that. The proof in the pudding was in the trot, though - I don't have the nicest trot to post but I have to say Chris Scarlett has taught her a thing or two - like how not to plop back down on my back like the Dow Jones in a deadfall, and how not to nag me with her lower leg. It was a lovely time, as it always is between two old friends who know and love each other dearly. We know each other's faults but love one another in spite of them. She was tearful when she got off - and she told me how sorry she was that she didn't learn these things sooner, and so sorry that her learning curve had been so hard on me. She wished she had been a better rider for me, because she knew I was trying as hard as I could to understand and be good for her. I just leaned my head into her as she scratched my ears (oh I so love when she scratches my ears!) and nuzzled her, which was my way of saying that there was no need to be apologetic for what she didn't know - I know in my heart she would walk through fire for me if she had to, there was never a doubt in my mind she did the best she could; she loved me enough to strive always to be better. Still, she said, we always wish we could have given our first horses the benefit of all we have learned on the horses who followed them. But thank you Bailey, for being a good sport and my best boy. She said if she ever needs to be reminded of what forgiveness and grace looks like, all she has to do is look at me. I told her that's right, but still don't forget to bring some carrots. Grace and forgiveness may be free - but tolerance carries a price!

January 31, 2014

The Daily Bailey

"Accept what is, let go of what was, and have faith in what will be." ~ unknown

Life is good today. While the eastern half of the country is a popsicle, it seems here in California we decided not to celebrate winter this year. Someone obviously forgot to inform my pituitary gland, which, because it didn't get the memo, has produced enough hair growth to give me a coat thick as a Tibetan yak - which Mom is furiously trying to shed out even as we speak. She swears I am growing it out as fast as she scrapes it off - as it is falling at my feet in clumps only to roll down the barn aisle like tumbleweed. She's using that sanding block thingy that feels soooo good on my old ribs and back. Some horses hate being curried, but I am not one of them. And even if I was, I would hold still today, because I can tell she needs a task to occupy her mind for a while. She proceeds to tell me she needs back surgery soon. When she does, she won't be able to come visit me for a few weeks, but don't worry, she has not abandoned me. Chris and Val and Mia will all look after me and make sure I stay vertical, keep my water bucket filled and call Dr. Sarah if I look unwell, and yes Mia will make sure I get my grain bucket at night. She says it takes a long time for the spine to heal, so they told her she couldn't ride for a whole year, and some doctors even said never because it might be too dangerous - but I just smiled when I heard that. They don't know my Mom. She said she is really scared some days, and often in a lot of pain. Recovering from that kind of surgery will be no picnic, and she has no idea what to expect. .She isn't sure if she will still have a lot of pain, of if she will ever be as active as she has up to now. Some days, she thinks there's no use hoping she will ever ride again. Oh my. No wonder she's in such a state. I wrapped my head around her and gently curried her shoulder with my teeth as she brushed my back. I used to do that all the time for Beckett, when his old joints ached, to take his mind off the pain and let him know I loved him. I wanted to tell her that, when I had laminitis, I didn't know either what was going to happen. I hurt badly. I didn't know if the pain would go away. I was scared if I couldn't do what I used to, she would give me away, or something even worse! But you know what? She promised me that no matter what, if I wanted to live, she would not give up on me - and she reminded me every day. It took almost two years, but in the end, I surprised them all. I did get better; I even took her cross-country again (much to the surprise of those who said never) and we felt blessed beyond measure. So, I say, how can anyone judge what greatness lies in a soul? About the time she realized what I was trying to tell her, she of course is crying. (the woman cries at the drop of a hat)

I proceed to remind her that if I, at the equivalent age of 70-something could come back from the brink of death like that, for God's sake take hold of yourself woman! Stop sniveling on my shoulder, put your big girl boots on and COWGIRL UP! There's work to be done! Besides - if your family can't use YOU at least you know they can't legally put you down! THAT made her laugh, which is far more like her, and ever so good to hear. Humans. They lack the ability to live in the moment like we horse do - a fact which sorely complicates their lives, if you ask me - but try telling them that. Days like this make me glad I am a horse. And by the looks of those carrots in the grain bucket, especially her horse.

March 1, 2014

The Daily Bailey

"Life is a tragedy to those who feel, but a comedy to those who think." ~Horace Walpole

Life is good today, but I think Mom is right. Just when you think you've seen all the crazy someone has to offer; you discover they have a hidden underground garage of crazy you never knew existed. This observation was prompted by the spook I threw in at the barbecue which has now taken up residence in the corner of the covered arena. Yes, you were correct in hearing the word barbecue in the same sentence as horse and covered arena. Apparently plans are in the work to use the covered arena as a giant grilling area for some rib cook-off for bikers. Now how safe, I ask you, can a horse feel in close proximity to fire, smoke, and the smell of charring animal flesh? Right? Mom just rolled her eyes and laughed, she says there's no use getting worked up, as you can't apply reason to a situation like this is like putting salve on a dead man. It's just no use. Best to apply liberal amounts of humor and wait for all to pass. Just the same, as I walked past this big red and silver animal flesh-charring contraption, I gave a good snort or two, just on principle. I suppose as long as they are not barbecuing horse meat, I will do as Mom recommends, and take it all in stride.

March 31, 2014

The Daily Bailey

"Accept the things to which fate binds you and love the people with whom fate brings you together but do so with all your heart." ~ Marcus Aurelius

Life is good today. The weather cannot make up its mind to be winter or spring, but at least the rain brought some respite from those damnable flies which are already beginning to annoy us. Mr. C went home yesterday, and I was a little sad to see him go if you can believe that. I know I was a bit jealous in the beginning - but I came to be quite fond of him in the end. I do, however, enjoy the fact that I am now the only horse in her life again. We got to spend most of the afternoon together, and she talked to me while she tried shedding out yet another layer of my winter coat. She was talking about fate, and said she once read that fate was like a strange restaurant, with odd little waiters who brought you things you never asked for and didn't always like. She says she certainly didn't ask for a serving of what she's got on her plate now but seeing as she can't send it back, she'll have to swallow it gracefully. I sometimes see Brandon give stuff he doesn't like to eat to the barn dogs. I don't suppose that is an option in this case. I did point out to her that while fate brought her to this place in time, it also brought her a lovely second horse - who in the short time he was here, taught her things she'd struggled for years to learn on me. And, in the process she got to meet Cheryl, and then her friend Tia, so her circle of horsewomen friends just expanded by two. Might it not be possible fate will bless her again even in the face of serious health problems? I know she is very worried about this upcoming spine surgery, but it is what it is. I reminded her how she often said our biggest blessings sometimes come disguised as disasters. Whether the currying had given her a channel to release her frustrations or she was just plain tired of being covered in my hair, I don't know. But as she blew the hair off her face for the umpteenth time, she finally admitted I was right.

April 5, 2014

The Daily Bailey

"To everything there is a season, and a time for every purpose under heaven." ~ Ecclesiastes

Life is good today. Mom says all good things must come to an end, and if it isn't good anymore it must be the end. Our lives have been a bit cattywampus lately; Mr. C has suffered a tendon tear, needing stem cell treatment and a year off in pasture so he can heal. The nagging back pain which has plagued Mom for months is finally making it almost impossible for her to ride anymore, anyway. There are days when she can hardly walk, even with a back brace. What with tendon tears and spine issues, what used to work well for us here now does not, and so we must find what does. Mr. C went back home, to a little red barn with goats, turkeys and chickens at a place owned by a friend of his Mom. He likes the goats I hear, but for the life of me, I can think of no reason a horse might need a goat to feel good. And don't go reminding me about Secretariat; those racehorses do a lot of dubious things from what I hear. I'm not so sure I want to leave here – after all I've got a penthouse of a stall with not one but two paddocks, but Mom says she's got me covered. She's already found a barn where I can still have a penthouse stall AND grass turnout every day, weather permitting, not only that, it's right across the aisle from Bel, the pretty dapple gray I know from the old neighborhood. Visitors are welcome there, so I hope Mom sent out notices – I'm sure many people would like to come visit and bring me carrots. The barn is only 3 miles from Mom's new house or her work, and she already knows some of the people who board there. She hates to move me again, but changes may be coming we need to plan for. And so, we begin a new chapter in our story; together, one step at a time.

April 17, 2014

The Daily Bailey

"Being afraid of the dark is what keeps most of us alive." ~ Edward Carnby, from Alone in the Dark, 2005

Life is good today. I was out in pasture all day with a little buckskin and a chestnut; both are good company even if they are not much to look at. One is named Bandit, and one they call Bob because they say he was Bought for One Buck because he was so homely. Mom doesn't think he is homely, but she's no reliable judge, she thinks even the mule is cute. Mom's dog Dakota got into BIG trouble today. Mom had him tied to the arena with a lead rope while we rode, which he somehow managed to undo, and bolted after the barn cat. Mom says it is because of something called high prey drive, but I personally think he has ADD and blame the fact he escaped on all those years of Pony Club training; I don't think Mom remembers how to tie anything besides a quick release knot. That ended our ride, but the sun was going down anyway, so it was as good a time as any to stop. As we were all being untacked and brushed, talk turned to how ironic it was that all of our moms are afraid of the dark, being as so much of what happens with horses in a barn happens IN the dark, especially when daylight savings ends. Mom confessed she talks to herself (and God) when she turns out the last barn light to walk the last 10 pitch black feet to the gate. Just once I wish I could talk like Mr. Ed and answer her. She admits to owning enough flashlights and lanterns to bring Air Force One down for an emergency night landing. So, if for some reason Travis Air Force base is closed, no need to worry, the POTUS is safe with us. Heather says if Mom is ever attacked, she can at least blind her assailant with one of the spotlights. As a horse, I can identify with those primal predatory fears; being a walking meal for predators higher up the food chain gives one a healthy respect for the dark and what lives in it. I had to laugh, though, when Mom said her dream barn would be lit up like Safeway with those lights like they have in the freezer section that turn on as you approach and turn off behind you as you do. Where on earth does she come up with these things?

July 13, 2014

The Daily Bailey

"A dog may be man's best friend, but the horse wrote history." ~ Jerry Smith

Life is good today. I am growing fat and dappled on all this grass, which has grown so tall in the pasture I hardly need to bend to graze. This suits me just fine as at my age, I have no need to expend needless energy. I like this place. Several of the horses are going to a show tomorrow, which means everyone will be astir early loading up to trailer out. I left them a good luck wish on the board, but I will be just as happy to sleep in. Mom still trims my mane and shaves off my old man whiskers – she says retirement is no excuse to let appearances slide. She brought that great dire wolf of a dog with her again, who she insists really is still just a puppy. For a dog, he's pretty smart, if you ask me. He figured out right quick that the horses who kick at the front of their stalls are being very ill-mannered and need to be barked at. Loudly. He has zero tolerance for horses that squeal at their neighbors and puts a quick stop to that as well. Smart as he is, he will never be as noble as a horse, and more's the pity. Perhaps Mom should park him down at the end of the barn aisle in front of those two sour little mares who pin their ears and lunge at people, teeth bared and glaring. I bet he'd take the piss and vinegar out of them right quick if he just bared his teeth back once. Though he is not a horse, he can still be useful I suppose. I am glad at times Mom cannot always read my mind.

August 13, 2014

The Daily Bailey

"Life is a shipwreck, but we must remember to sing in the lifeboats." ~ Voltaire

Life is good today. Roger is doing such a great job on my feet; my shoeing is the envy of the barn. That man certainly knows how to set back a toe. We went out on trail with the new horse, Dakota, and rode around the orchards near the barn. Being thoroughbreds, both us were all fired up as we were certain snarks and grumpkins were behind every tree. Mom said if everyone knew how good riding was for the soul, therapists would go broke. The world is a troubled place these days. Ebola has become an epidemic in Africa, ISIS is beheading any Christian who refuses to convert to Islam, and Robin Williams, one of the most gifted and talented comedians has committed suicide. If he, who could find the comic relief in any situation could not be happy, what does that portend for the rest of us? She wishes all troubled souls could find their way to horses, as she is convinced it would heal them somehow. Barn chores do tend to keep one grounded, I suppose. There is a comforting and tedious rhythm to them Mom says unravels all the knots the day puts into her. Bailey, she said, when the world is going to hell in a handbasket, horses help us to find our way out of the basket and keep us keeping on. I have no idea what hell or handbaskets are, but I am very glad I keep her out of them.

August 17, 2014

The Daily Bailey

"Eternally woman spills herself away in driblets to the thirsty, seldom being allowed the time, the quiet, the peace to let the pitcher fill up to the brim." ~ Anne Morrow Lindbergh

Life is good today. It is my first girl Heather's 30th birthday! Oh, how I have missed her and our adventures! Mom would never let me gallop as fast as Heather did – we were a force to be reckoned with, for sure. Heather is somewhere Mom calls Back East, which seems very far away, but I hear she is doing very well on her new mare Mattie. I am so happy for her. I hope she comes to visit soon, as I want to hear all about how the cross-country courses ride Back East. Today, I gave another mom her very first riding lesson, and oh how happy I was to hear Chris's calm and steady voice in the ring again. This mom is a friend of my Mom, and I kind of like her because she is very kind and soft with me and takes her time with things. A horse can always tell if one truly has a love for animals, and this woman does. She's still learning to put the halter and bridle on, so I'm very patient with her, and try to lower my head at the proper time to help her out. Even though I am retired, I still like having a job and this one seems just right. Chris says there's a lot I can teach her without working too hard. Mom is happy to share me, and happier still should her friend discover how good riding is for the soul, if not the pocketbook. I'm just happy to be vertical and productive, given my advanced age. And if that means helping someone fill their pitcher to the brim, well then, I'm happy to do it. Life is very very good today. Happy 30th birthday Heather from your first One-Star horse!

September 22, 2014

The Daily Bailey

"Every survival kit should come with a sense of humor" ~ unknown.

Life is good today. Finally overheard some news about Mom by eavesdropping on Val as she updated the barn crew. I've been so worried about her because I can hear her calling to me, but I can't get to her. Val says she ended up back in the hospital again because she passed out in the x-ray room and turned blue and then they called a Code Blue, whatever that was. Val says Mom figured it wasn't her time to go because she didn't see the white light or the tunnel, and Beckett wasn't there to meet her, and she knows Beckett would never break his promise. Mom said she could hear everything, and strangest part was hearing the overhead page and realizing SHE was the Code Blue. She remembers thinking OK, that means a whole bunch of people will be running to me in minutes, if I can hang on til then please God give me the best ED doc there is. Poor Debra who took her in got the fright of her life and may need therapy after witnessing all of this. Mom told Val she had officially sunken to her lowest when she realized not only do they have signs posted that she is a fall risk, they even put a bed alarm on her in case she tried to get up by herself in the night. That made me laugh. Mom is more like Blanche from Golden Girls; any problems involving bed have nothing to do with getting out of bed. She says she must wear a back brace that makes her look like a Ninja turtle, and that, on top of needing a walker for balance, is just going a little too far. Here she was hoping the hardware in her back would require pat downs by TSA agents. If I were a TSA agent, the last person I'd want to pat down is a granny in a brace with a walker. Might find me one of those ostomy bags! I heard Val say what caused all the ruckus was something that sounded like Sinking Pee, but I don't know what that is. Good Lord I hope she doesn't need diapers too - that Devocoux saddle will need to be a bit bigger. Bel, who has better hearing than I do explained no, it wasn't sinking pee, it was syncope. Mom had simply passed out and stopped breathing because the pain medication was too strong for her, I listened quietly while eating my hay about how the many friends and patients who she's helped in the past came to help her when she couldn't help herself. I wish I could be there for her; I know I'd make her feel better.

I am glad she has people around her to love her through this -I wish I could tell them all how very grateful I am. But only Mom and Chris know I can talk. Val says she brought her home today so maybe she will come and visit me soon. I send her horse thoughts, but I don't know if humans receive them the same as we animals do. If you know her, let her know I love her, and I will be right here waiting for her just like she was for me.

September 24, 2014

The Daily Bailey

Piglet sidled up to Pooh from behind. "Pooh" he whispered. " Yes Piglet?" "Nothing" said Piglet, taking Pooh's paw. "I just wanted to be sure of you". ~AA Milne

Life is good today! Mom came for a visit! I guess Eva felt sorry for her after she burst into tears hearing the doctor wouldn't allow her to drive for 4 more weeks...and so she said grab the bag of carrots, dry your eyes and get in, we're going. I was so happy to hear her voice! But I did not at all like that black metal thing she was wearing - in fact I turned my butt to her as soon as she stepped into my stall. Until she explained that this is the way it had to be for the next few months, if she was ever going to heal properly to ride again. And then, she reached up and scratched both my ears and I forgot all about how funny it looked; and after a few carrots I even chanced a nibble at it. I don't know what Velcro is, but it doesn't taste good. Mom got to meet the new mare at the barn, Athena, and Dakota hung out watching over it all. I got my ears scratched, my face washed, my tail brushed, and Eva picked my feet for me. Mom says now she has metal plates and screws in her spine, and she's thinking of patenting a super magnet to build into a saddle which will keep her in it. How about that for a woman with too much time on her hands? Well, she says, they are already using a similar principle with stirrups, so it isn't impossible, until I reminded her that those gimmicks were invented for people who never learned to keep their heels down. Oh, yeah, she says. I guess you're right. Of course I'm right, I'm a horse! She stood next to me for a long time, just leaning on me and putting her arms as far around as they would go; she says she'll get out as often as she can get a ride, and be patient because 4 weeks isn't that long after all. I nuzzled her shoulder and told her there is no rush. I will be right here.

October 20, 2014 ·

The Daily Bailey

"Find out where joy resides and give it a voice far beyond singing. For to miss the joy is to miss all." ~ Robert Louis Stevenson

Life is good today. Cooler weather is setting in, and I no longer have to stand for hours in front of my stall fan for relief from the heat. Bel, just back from Fresno Horse Park, says Goose and Cheryl had good rides, although I think Boleybawn's Andy should be sold to the Amish for a plow horse because he was such a hooligan. Tantzie was out to ride Shelby's horse T, and she looks just right on him. I am trying to be ever so patient with Georgina as she learns how to post the trot, because I do like how she fusses over me. She was so happy after practice Friday she was singing a song about Anna's Oreos. How riding made her happy enough to sing about cookies escaped me, until Mom explained no, not Anna's Oreos, anaorios, which is Spanish for carrots. That's more like it, I thought. Mom laughed, and said it was good to see her so full of joy and a sense of accomplishment. Mom told Georgina this was a sure sign her husband was now doomed to the equestrian life, but there are worse fates in life. As a horse, I must agree.

November 27, 2014

The Daily Bailey

"There are things you do because they feel right and they may make no sense and they may make no money and it may be the real reason we are here: to love each other and to eat each other's cooking and say it was good." ~ Brian Andreas

Life is good today. The pastures have some new green grass from earlier rains, and while our people are enjoying meals with dear ones, we are enjoying peace, quiet, warm sun and good grass. We have much to be thankful for this year. Even though she still needs to wear a funny-looking brace, Mom's surgery has taken away her back pain and she can even stand up straight again. My teeth, though a bit loose in the front, still work well enough to keep me fat and sassy which is pretty good for a pensioner of my age. At 24, I'm the equivalent of an 80-year-old. You couldn't get Georgina to believe that, as she has seen me on one of my most, shall we say, 'sparkly' days. I can still act like a teenager at times. Mom says the short stories she wrote about our horse adventures were very well-reviewed - and may very well be published by this time next year! She's dedicating this book to me and Beckett, because if it wasn't for us, she never would have started writing them. I hope they put a picture of me and Beckett on the cover. We are such handsome horses after all.

And would you believe this - Mom says we now have our own business! She calls it the Desperate Horsewyfe and she IS using my favorite picture of me and her as the business logo. She showed me some of the things she will be selling - vases with horseshoes on them, saddle pads with bling, ornaments and other stuff. They look like they'd be fun to make if I had opposable thumbs, which I don't. She says she has to find some way to support us in our retirement or we will both be eating cat food and I may be living in the spare bedroom after grazing the back yard bare. Mom says loving horses is definitely one of those things that makes no money and sometimes no sense, but it feels right, and she wouldn't trade it for anything. And for that, I am thankful. Happy Thanksgiving to all humans and the horses who love them.

December 19. 2014

The Daily Bailey

"A man is not old until his regrets take the place of dreams." ~John Barrymore, "Good Night, Sweet Prince" 1943

Life is good today. It has been raining cats and dogs for days, which is good for next year's hay crop but for this year's horses, not so much. The younger ones are going a little stir-crazy in their confinement, and I chuckle when I see them let loose in the arena, leaving the gate like a bottle rocket - spinning and bucking for all they're worth. At my ripe old age, a few days of being cooped up is not the issue it used to be, especially since I have a double stall to wander around in. Speaking of ripe old ages, it was my Mom's birthday today! When she stopped by to put my jammies on, she said she got the best birthday present ever. Oh? I said, thoughtfully chewing on some teff hay. Well first of all, I'm still here, she said, which is a blessing in and of itself; less than 8 weeks ago, it was not looking like such a sure thing. Second, she said the spine surgeon officially cleared her to ride me again - just at the walk and taking it ever so easy but no matter, it's a start. It will be the better part of a year or more before she can do any jumping or even think about competition, but she's already planning on getting back into lessons and working hard on her flatwork. She laughed and said she may be the only competitor in the USEA to qualify for Social Security before she makes it out of the Beginner Novice division. It doesn't matter, I told her, what matters is that you still want to try. She nodded, and said she read once that we grow old by giving up our ideals, not by how many years we live; years wrinkle the face, she said, but giving up enthusiasm wrinkles the soul. She looked me square in the eye and said Bailey, I am not leaving this earth with an old wrinkled soul. She said her Aunt Marge is 91 and still going strong, so she has no reason to believe that she didn't get some of those genes as well. Probly the same ones linked to the gene for stubbornness and attitude, I thought, but I didn't say that out loud. She scratched my ears and gave me a hug before she said goodnight, and told me rest up, 'cause baby we still got dreams!

December 31, 2014

The Daily Bailey

"And now we welcome the new year, full of things that have never been" ~ Rainer Maria Rilke

Life is good today. We have passed the shortest day of the year, and we are settled in to wait for the spring. I got the best Christmas present - my first girl Heather came to visit me! she was teaching a little girl on a white pony who wasn't much older than she was at the time she began competing. Mom says she has a big chestnut mare named Mattie now, but I still remember how we would fly along the prelim course while my Mom prayed fervently God would bring us both over the finish line at the same time and unharmed. She had no reason to worry, I would have jumped the moon for that girl. I showed her I still had some of that old sparkle as she trotted me around the ring for old time's sake. My we were quite the pair. Mom says today is the last day of the year, and we have much to celebrate. We are both happy and healthy, we have friends who love us, and enough food to eat. We are blessed, and grateful for all that has happened in this past year, the good and the not so good as one helps us appreciate the other. We are also thankful to the people who have walked with us on this year's journey. I am especially grateful for the nice teff hay I am enjoying here, and a nice big stall to roam around in. Happy New Year everybody.

February 28, 2015

The Daily Bailey

"As I leave the barn, I take with me a renewed view, and a quiet soul" ~ unknown

Life is good today. The grass is new and green and the weather for now has turned warmer. We are all shedding like mad, and great balls of horsehair are rolling down the barn aisles like tumbleweed on windy days. Mom's still just able to walk around on me, but she says it's her saving grace. She says she doesn't remember a time in her life now that horses and what they needed were not at the center of it - starting with Heather and Ryan's first riding lesson. Little did she know then what this would lead to! And most days, she's very glad of it. When her soul is unsettled, and troubled with sadness for the struggles of friends, she finds great comfort here. There is a rhythm to a horsewoman's life that, while the rest of life goes to hell in a handbasket, remains simple, steady and constant: horses need to be fed, watered and groomed, exercised, and groomed again. stalls must be mucked out. tack must be cleaned. She says she can't explain why doing those chores quiets her mind, it just does. And today, her heart is very heavy; a dear friend has lost her only daughter, and more than a few of Mom's friends are facing the imminent death of their own dear friends, whom she does not know, to cancer. She tells me the stories of these things as she brushes me, while she tacks me up. I don't know any of these people, but I hear the grief in Mom's voice as she speaks of their respective trials - and her prayers for them – and I realize she must love them very much. I know by the time she is ready to saddle up, she will be all talked out and we can have a lovely ride in the afternoon sun, just her and me. It has been this way with the two of us for so many years now, I almost don't remember a time when I wasn't hers. Bailey, she says, I am a firm believer that the reason we are all here is just to walk each other home; they don't tell you ahead of time how hard that walk may be. But, she says, as she rubs my ears (oh how I love this!) - it's who you take along on the journey that makes all the difference.

March 21, 2015

The Daily Bailey

"Stay close to anything that makes you glad you are alive." ~ Hafiz

Life is good today. Spring is upon us! The days are hot, but not hot enough yet to breed a troublesome number of flies; horses enjoy this temporary blessing. A big old barn owl has taken up residence in the rafters of our indoor; scaring the hell out of poor Cindy the other night when he abruptly left his perch. She didn't know owls had such a huge wingspan. Mom would like him to follow her home and roost in her rafters, as he could quickly end the pigeon problem in the neighborhood. She says pigeons are vermin dressed in feathers. I'm not sure what vermin are, but clearly it is undesirable to her. We have been having a great time since she was cleared to come back and ride again - even though we work mostly at the walk. Chris says I still have a lot to teach her, and while I do enjoy being back to light work again, we are both a little older and stiffer than we used to be. We often ride to music, which mostly I like because it helps Mom keep steady rhythm and her hands don't bounce so much. She talks to me while we ride and talks to herself a lot - which I also find entertaining. You never know what might come out of that woman's mouth! Last night, for instance, she was playing some Latin ballroom music - Oh God, I thought, here we go again with that garrocha business. (the last time she rode to that music she thought it would be a grand idea to make me walk and canter around a 12-foot lunge whip, in between dragging it alongside me and passing it over her head - what was she thinking?) The whites of my eyes started to show the moment I heard flamenco guitar, and shortly thereafter, castanets. Castanets! is this woman mad? And then, in her best Skippy Jon Jones voice she begins telling me how we are in Jerez de La Frontera, on our way to a feria, and we must show our very best walk so the ladies will throw roses at us and cheer for us. And with that she legs me into a very nice and forward walk - and I can almost hear toreador music in the distance. I put my very best swagger into this walk, which soon becomes a slow trot because I just can't help myself. Mom, instead of stopping me, starts to laugh and says 'OK, let's go with this' and for the first time in more than a year, is actually sitting the trot, and to my surprise, sitting it well. And laughing! This is no small accomplishment - if you know me, you know my trot is not one of my best gaits. No amount of latin ballroom music or castanets is going to improve on that - but as I remind her, I am a thoroughbred, not an andalusian. Still, I have to admit I was inspired in that direction for a moment. Someone once said about my mom 'Follow the laughter and you'll usually find Dawn right in the middle of it'. Now I see why - she seems to have the ability to find the fun in almost anything. It's a good quality to have in this life, I think.

Later as she brushes me and tucks me in for the night she tells me she never thought she'd be happy to sit the trot, especially my trot, but it feels so good to be doing what she loves again, especially with me - she tells me " It keeps us young, Bailey, at least young at heart". And you know, I have to agree.

May 2, 2015 ·

The Daily Bailey

"On old horses you learn how to ride" ~German proverb

Life is good today. We've all enjoyed a good turn out in the pastures today and for some of us, not a moment too soon. Odin has been rattling his bucket to keep himself entertained in his confinement as the pastures were irrigated, which startles the mares and sets them on edge. Being only four, he thinks this is great fun. The folly of youth. At my age, I know better than to stir up the mares. We've had some lovely rides this past week - all starting with our lesson last Monday. Mom's been working on leg yields, shoulder in and haunches in - talk about going back to basics. She read somewhere that it takes a thousand repetitions before something you learn becomes automatic - which means, she says, we have a lot of work ahead of us. We? I already know how to do these things; she on the other hand, needs to practice how to ask. I remind her that I am a thoroughbred, not a mind-reader. She laughs and admits that I am right, which of course I am. I am also not the one with the spatial issue, who can't remember which leg needs to be behind the girth or ahead of the girth, which seat bone needs to be weighted for the movement in question, or which way the horse needs to be bent accordingly. She sighs. It's a good thing we are both old and patient and at least one of us knows what we should be doing! She is ever so glad Heather passed me on to be her teacher - and I confess, so am I. It isn't that I didn't love what I did for Heather – I was quite competitive in my younger years and nothing felt better than making it 'round that course double clear. We certainly were a force to be reckoned with. But it was hard work preparing and training, and at this age I find I do not miss the pressure of needing to be at the peak of my game. I am quite content with the less demanding task of helping Mom master the skills which will make her a better rider. I may be her old horse, but as she points out, she's not so young either, and we both have lots to offer one another. And she's happy for it. Bailey, she says, you are first in my heart because you've taught me, I can trust you to be my teacher. For an old horse, I'd say that's a pretty good place to be.

May 9, 2015

The Daily Bailey

"Everything should be made as simple as possible, but no simpler." ~Albert Einstein

Life is good today. Bel is flirting shamelessly with all of us geldings these days, being in season, which causes all of us to neigh anxiously after her whenever she is out of sight. Gelding us didn't leave us blind, you know. She loves us now but, in a few weeks, she won't give us the time of day, so we are taking advantage of her hormonal good humor. I think I'm making progress teaching Mom to ask for what she wants clearly and correctly. As Val says, a thoroughbred will always give you 110% of what you ask for - so if you ask wrong, be prepared for 110% of what you didn't want. The problem is, the woman thinks too much sometimes. She tries to weight the correct seat bone and apply the correct aid timed when the appropriate hind leg is leaving the ground, make sure her shoulders are square with mine, hold the outside rein and all the while keep me in front of her leg. Unless you are Lilo Fore or Steffan Peters, I don't know if that means bend, go sideways, forward, whhhaaaaatt??? I think Chris has finally impressed upon her the value of keeping it simple - starting with legs in the right position, long and not squeezing me like a sausage casing. Keep your outside leg slightly back of the girth, and inside leg at the girth. All the aids we are working at for these exercises are applied from this position it is the way they are delivered, that is the ticket. Stop hopping from one seat bone to another, forcing your shoulders by twisting your body. Relax for God's sake. this isn't rocket science, it's a leg yield. And there, didn't we get a nice round and forward trot out of that? I would like to thank Chris except I had a good thing going dragging her around the ring like a cart horse - she wouldn't put me in front of her leg because she thought I was tired, and old, and felt sorry she had to pull me from retirement to rehab through her back surgery. And quite frankly I would have taken advantage of her soft heart as long as I could. I don't care how much those natural horsemen talk about joining up and being one with the leader; I have never met a horse that said "Oh, yes, please, let's put that heavy dressage saddle on and I want to go around in circles at a very collected trot; you wait here, I'll get the girth. " BAHAHAHA! Thankfully just as Mom was discussing the use of spurs or a dressage whip, Chris again points out the simpler option - which was a good thump with both legs. Now THAT got me moving forward with a capital F. Teaching my Mom has been a long slow process, and the learning curve has more often been harder on me, but I will give her credit for this - she tries with all her heart to learn how to give a horse the best ride - and though she falls short of the mark at times, she doesn't give up, she just tries again. She may be my Mom, but she's definitely got my same thoroughbred heart.

June 7, 2015

The Daily Bailey

"We leave something of ourselves behind when we leave a place, we stay there, even though we go away. And there are things in us that we can find again only by going back there." ~unknown

Life is good today. Pastures are being irrigated, so we are all confined to quarters for a few days. This is hardest on the youngsters, like Odin, who is beginning to crib on the lower edge of the grill on his stall. I have a bigger stall to roam around in and for this I am grateful. Also, for the fans, which keep both the air and the flys moving. I think Mom's been really homesick these past few months - she's asked me how I'd like being an East coast horse and talks about Pennsylvania. I'm not sure I'd like the winters there, but home is wherever she is, so if she goes, I go. She laughs at herself for even thinking of it - she told me a woman named Beryl Markham once wrote 'if you have to leave a place where all your yesteryears are buried, you should leave it the fastest way you can, and never go back.' I think she misses her sisters and brothers, a problem I don't have, as an only child. I've actually met three of her sisters - they were lovely women - kind, generous with a carrot, and quite funny. It's no wonder she misses their company. She says California has never felt like home, though she has come to have some dear, dear friends here. But home doesn't feel like home anymore, either, just familiar. I think she should buy herself a cute little summer cottage on some property, put up a barn and be a snowbird. Go back to Pennsylvania for summers and fall, and then head back here to winter over. That seems the best of both worlds. And avoids the issue of me having to wear 3 blankets like I hear MacGregor and Mattie do in those stone-cold New England winters. No ma'am, I'll stay a California horse, thank you, and if she's smart, she'll stay a California girl. This feeling will pass. She needs a visit, not a life change. It won't take her long to realize home is people, not a place. It's wherever the people and the dog and the horse who love you are, building memories with you, that, piece by piece, form a solid shelter around you that you take with you wherever you go.

June 28, 2015

The Daily Bailey

" Tolerance implies no lack of commitment to one's own beliefs. Rather it condemns the oppression or persecution of others". ~John F. Kennedy

Life is good today. Rainbows everywhere, as far as the eye can see. Mom says it's because of something called a SCOTUS ruling. As she was brushing me, she chuckled and said that while most of the country is celebrating, some are gnashing their teeth, convinced we are on the path to perdition headed straight to hell. She told me that's what they said in the 60's, too, about listening to rock and roll, especially the Rolling Stones, so she isn't worried. She says the ruling doesn't affect us in any way, and she still considers herself married to her horse (which is currently me) regardless of what the courts say. As it should be, I say. Being a particularly well-read horse, I do know there are other more ridiculous laws which should draw the ire of those who profess to be concerned about our eternal salvation. Did you know, for example, there are states in which conjugal relations with animals are legal? How can that bring anyone closer to God, I wonder. Can an animal, like an adult, legally give meaningful consent? Good thing I am a horse and not an attorney. Still, one wonders at the absurdity of it all. As we walked around the indoor, Mom reached over and gave me a pat. She said she wished I could read Justice Kennedy's opinion - it was such a powerful and articulate explanation of the majority's decision - it made her cry. Bailey my boy, she said, sometimes the only place life makes sense is right here in the barn. You know why Bailey? Because in spite of all the other nonsense that goes on in the rest of the world, in here, #lovewins.

July 18, 2015

The Daily Bailey "Silly people say stupid things; clever people do them." ~Marie Von Ebner-Eschenbach

Life is good today. I have developed a new empathy for women who as part of their dress, must wear pantyhose. How, you may ask, did this come about? Because my Mom, in her frantic mission to relieve this damnable headshaking I've developed, read somewhere that placing a nylon stocking over my muzzle would help. Yes, you read correctly. A stocking. And since she had no trouser length stocking, she felt reasonable to substitute a thigh-high stockkng with one of those fancy lace tops, figuring she would just tie a knot in the end to make it the appropriate length. Which explains why Cheryl came into the barn to see my muzzle dressed like a french whore in elasticized lace, flipping my head up and down with the knotted stocking dangling from the end of my nose like an elephant's trunk. I don't know what was funnier - the horrified expression on her face or Mom, trying not to pee her pants as she was laughing so hard. Thankfully, this was swiftly dismissed as a viable therapeutic option. What possessed her, I wonder, to believe compressing my nose with a foundation undergarment would somehow be helpful? She says she read that it would help over-ride the impulses my eyes were giving the trigeminal nerve, causing me to flip my head violently up and down. I politely reminded her not to believe everything she reads, even if she does find it with Google. She agreed, thankfully, to continue managing this new health problem conservatively. While distracting and distressful to watch as well as experience (it feels like bugs are crawling all over my face) it is not fatal, and we don't want the cure to be worse than the disease. She brings me out in evening hours when the light is low, as the light does set me off a great deal. Such is the nature of devoted friends. Next week, we will give the cold laser a try, as this has been successful in people with trigeminal nerve issues. I heard when they used it on Twoey, it put her to sleep it felt so good. It may not help but at least it won't hurt and does not involve the wearing of foundation garments.

August 8, 2015

The Daily Bailey

“What is a teacher? I'll tell you: it isn't someone who teaches something, but someone who inspires the student to give of her best...” ~Paulo Coelho, The Witch of Portobello

Life is good today. I am so proud of my first girl, Heather. Mom told me all Heather's students did very well at their shows this weekend - with Nina earning the best dressage score she's ever had and Julia winning some championship mom can't remember the name of to save her life. There were also some winning rides in the hunter/jumper rings, but Mom can't keep the names of those classes straight either. She really enjoys hearing about the young riders Heather is bringing along, and how they are progressing. If she didn't live on the opposite coast, she swears she would adopt them all and become the official barn mom. She's always wanting to make them saddle pads, or T-shirts, or something small to celebrate their efforts and cheer them on. Sometimes I miss the rides I had with Heather - we were quite a team in my younger days. She has a gift for inspiring trust and confidence in horses - I'm not surprised it's carried over to her students.

I hope she comes to visit me if she comes home for Christmas, so I can tell her myself how proud I am that she is passing on that passion for excellence she carries. Well done Heather, and a salute to all your riders who did so well this weekend. Come see a fat old man one day, and bring him a carrot, would you?

September 23, 2015

The Daily Bailey

"The art of medicine consists in amusing the patient while nature cures the disease." ~ Voltaire

Life is good today. The days are getting shorter and a little cooler, and I have renewed hope that this damnable headshaking may be amenable to the most interesting of remedies. Dr. Sarah stopped by the other day with the UC Davis team to see if she could help, and sure enough she thinks that something called counter-stimulation may trick my facial nerves into ignoring the impulse to electrify my face every time I'm exposed to bright sunlight. The whole process was quite entertaining at least for the observers - I, however, did not enjoy being led around with a surgical towel draped from the noseband of my halter looking for all the world like Barbara Eden in I Dream of Jeannie. Entirely unbefitting a noble breed such as the thoroughbred. I wonder what William R. Pritchard would think of that. He'd be horrified, I am sure. It could be worse, however. I overheard Dr. Sarah telling Mom that one woman actually put a black lace bra over her horse's eyes to filter out the light. My Mom does not need any brighter ideas like this. Do we not recall the epic failure of the pantyhose over the nose trial? For now, we are trying the special noseband that goes with my UV fly mask, which makes me look like Atom Ant with full face armor. If this doesn't work, we get to try something made of dangling pieces of knotted leather shoelaces which will hang down in front of my nose from the noseband of my bridle or halter. Sweet mother of Jesus let the face mask work! I can at least pretend it is a chamfron and take comfort in the illusion of dignity; an impossibility when one has dangling pieces of leather flapping about like fringe from your halter. I will be the laughingstock of the barn. Mom says no matter, we will do whatever works and keeps me comfortable. She says we've been figuring out how to work with each other since Heather passed me on to her, and she sees no reason to give up now, being as we've come so far. Even if she could never ride me again, she won't give up until she figures out how she can help. I do love the fact that she loves me so dearly, but please God, I hope she doesn't own any black lace bras.

November 3, 2015 ·

The Daily Bailey

"Being deeply learned and skilled, being well trained and using well spoken words: this is good luck." ~ Buddha

Life is good today. The past two days have been cloudy and gray, so my face doesn't feel like it's electrified; and as a result, I gave Mom two really great rides which we both deeply appreciated. She's wanted to ride more often than I could accommodate her with this darn head-shaking thing, but the past two rides more than made up for it. I helped her practice her half-halts, which are one of the most notoriously subtle, difficult to teach, and necessary skill a rider must acquire. Mom's convinced that this is in part, because describing how to ride a half halt is like describing pornography. You'll know it when you see it - or feel it, I guess. Do you know how many ways there are to interpret 'deepen your seat'? what does that even mean? Mom says a seat can only go so far into a saddle so does it mean sit harder? no, the dressage masters tell us to emphasize 'the swing' of the seat in any gait. One is not supposed to tighten the thigh, but we are supposed to apply the lower leg (ever so softly as to encourage the horse's hindquarters to engage) and FOR GOD'S SAKE DON'T PULL BACK ON THE REINS. She says when she figures this out, she is sure that she will be able to translate the Dead Sea Scrolls from Sanskrit - it must be easier than this. Fortunately, being the ancient but willing schoolmaster, I am, I was happy to help. Being an exquisitely sensitive and well-trained thoroughbred, it only took me a few trips around the ring to teach her the basics of timing and application of the aids. She's not fluid at it by any means (subtle is not in the woman's skill set) but she's better than was, and this is all that matters - she'll work on it until she gets it. She told me I have no idea how different it is riding another breed when you are used to a thoroughbred. That little medicine paint she rode in Connecticut. OMG Bailey, I was straining so hard to engage my core it's a wonder I didn't prolapse an intestine. And nothing! no slowing down, no indication whatsoever I was even up there in the saddle. So, I tried a different approach. Some people describe engaging the core like 'bearing down' So I bear down and tighten my abdominal muscles - still nothing. I didn't work this hard delivering two babies! So how then do I deepen my seat? do I squeeze with inner thigh? hip adductors? inner calf? no that's supposed to ever so gently encourage the hind-quarters, which are now western jogging around the arena full of hunter jumpers who I am sure are snickering at me by now as they realize my daughter the trainer did NOT inherit her riding ability from me. If you squeeze with the wrong muscles you pop out of the saddle instead going deeper, whatever that means, and by God the hindquarters are going but certainly not engaged and how does this all work again? And then it all skids to a complete halt as in desperation I commit the atrocity I have been warned not to do - I pull back on the reins. Hard. But we at least halt. Oh God, Bailey, I was a hot mess - Heather was trying, I was trying, the horse was trying - there was no lack of effort and yet I just couldn't get it, she said, shaking her head as she curried me out. The benefit of experience, my dear, I gently reminded her. The medicine paint was a western horse first. I know they say it shouldn't matter but I sometimes disagree. When the rider doesn't know how to ask and the horse is not sure what the question is, sometimes it's helpful having a horse good at guessing the answer based on past experience. Granted not always, but in this instance, my educated guess helped you develop a better feel for not only application of the aids but with timing. In any case, I was glad to be back in the tack doing with you what I do best - patiently (well, mostly) teaching you what I've learned so you are that much better for the next horse. It's what I call job security.

January 8, 2016

The Daily Bailey

"Do not cast me off in the time of old age; forsake me not when my strength is spent." ~Psalm 71:9

Life is good today. Mom has a few more gray hairs and another bill from field service, I have a diaper duct taped to the sole of my left front foot, but for the shape we are in, we are in good shape. She knows at the ripe old age of 25, I'm getting a bit tired. Lord knows I never planned to stay this long, but here I am thanks to the love I have for her and my first girl. So, when the call came from the barn today that I was quite uncomfortable and had some heat in my front feet, she was prepared for the worst. She reminded me that if I needed to go home, I should go. After all, I've done more for her and Heather than she could ever repay. While we waited for field service, she asked me if I remembered all the rides where I taught her, she could trust me on the cross-country course, and how I absolutely took care of her. As I rested my head against her shoulder, she whispered in my ear that when the time comes, Bailey, it will be my turn to repay the favor; I will take care of you. I'm a nurse, she said, and I know how these things go; you can trust me, Bailey. I will carry you, just like you carried me. You will never believe what she said next. She said when I am reborn, I should come to her and let her know where I am, so she can come and get me so we could be together again - she said Margie told her to tell me this. And she said if I couldn't find her, I should talk to Margie, who knows me, and she will help me. Just please, if you have any say in the matter, try not to come back as a cat, a chihuahua, or a reptile. It would be really hard to love you if you were that, Bailey. But, she said, feel free to come back as a fat and mischievous pony who will carry my grandbabies around - that would be quite nice... Who knew? Thankfully today was not the day either one of us had to make those sorts of decisions. So far it seems like a simple abscess and not founder. Roger pulled my shoe, the field service poulticed my foot, and after a dose of banamine, I got turned out in the indoor and had myself a good buck and a roll before Mom tucked me in for the night. I'm glad it seems to be nothing more, and to know my place in her life does not depend on what I can still do for her. It is enough for me to nicker when she comes into the barn and doze off while she rubs my ears and scratches my neck. It is enough for her to drink in the smell of my coat and listen to the whoosh of my breath as she rests her cheek against my shoulder. I am enough. Still, I do like the idea of coming back to her one day, not in this old and tired body, so we can have many more adventures. Yes, life is good today.

February 2, 2016

The Daily Bailey

"Daughters do wonderful things. Not just the wonderful things you expected them to do. Different things. Astonishing things. Better than you ever dreamed." ~ Pamela Brown

Life is good today. My foot is all better, and Roger puts my shoe back on today. Mom says not a moment too soon, after watching me buck and squeal and snort all around the indoor last night. I was flirting with the new paint mare from RanchoTel. Well they said she was paint but she's hooded and blanketed like someone ready for germ warfare, so I can't really tell. But she does have pretty eyes. Mom says my first girl is in Ocala! She took Swell and Mattie and a couple of other horses down to work and train and compete for a month. My goodness look how far she's come! Can it be so long ago we were cruising around prelim? I'm so proud of her! I admit, it was hard at first when she had to move on to another horse. But horses know that sometimes, they only get to carry you for a part of your journey. She saw something in me that nobody else did, standing out in the field all scruffy and muddy - when everyone else looked past me, she saw straight to my heart and I never let her down. Denny Emerson is right- sometimes the scruffy horse standing out in the pasture really is the best horse for the job! I'm glad I carried her for as long as I did - I really couldn't ask for a better life. I hope Swell is a good boy for her, and Mattie behaves herself. Ride with all your heart, Heather - just like we did at Galway. You are braver than you believe, stronger than you think, and loved more than you'll ever know.

February 22, 2016

The Daily Bailey

"You are never too old to set a new goal or dream a new dream." ~ CS Lewis

Life is good today. Mom is in Florida visiting my first girl and she tells me Heather has a new horse named Rather Swell. Mattie, her mare, is down there as well, who Mom says is just as wicked ornery as ever. When you blanket her, Mom says she pins her ears and glares at you, gnashing her teeth in the air - because she's only made the mistake of biting Heather once. Now there is a match made in heaven if ever there was one. Mom told me they went to try a few horses today, and that she got to meet Bruce Davidson himself. He told her he knows of a woman who is 69 years old and just now decided to take up the sport of eventing. Mom laughed when she told me she might be that old, too, by the time she found the right horse to try such shenanigans again. I have a feeling she'll come upon the right lad to take up where I've left off - like falling in love it may happen when you least expect it. I look forward to hearing all about her adventures when she returns and settling in for a good scratch of the withers and a carrot.

March 13, 2016

The Daily Bailey "Never attribute to malice that which can adequately be explained by stupidity." ~ Robert J. Hanlon

Life is good today. A bit soggy, with all the rain, but overall, good. Mom says she is thoroughly disgusted with something called politics today, insisting they should be sending Denny Emerson and Jimmy Wofford to the electoral college as presidential candidates. She can just imagine what Denny might do with something called entitlement programs. She thinks George Morris should run for Senator as he'd make a rather handy majority whip. She must be pretty hot about all of this, as I distinctly noticed her currying becoming more animated with each name, she ticked off the list of candidates vying for the ticket. I would probably be missing a layer of skin if Cheryl hadn't walked in, which got her off the subject of politics and onto the meaning of a cryptic entry she had seen on our whiteboard. Why, Mom asks, are the words 'Barn Sour Bitches' written up there? Are you mad at us? Are you talking about all the moody mares? Or are we voting on a new team name? Well come to find out, this was how we (the boarders in general) were described earlier today - in the course of a heated dispute over property which thankfully Mom nor I was involved in. Listening to the details of today's ordeal, she just shook her head and laughed, glad she wasn't the one who had to endure it, although very empathetic to those who did. Mom offered to print up T-shirts for the boarders, complete with a Barn Sour Bitches logo across the front. This made everyone laugh and realize that truly, one had to keep a good sense of humor about the whole matter. Later she thought what an excellent signature cocktail this could be: The Barn Sour Bitch - 2 oz whiskey (preferably a good bourbon) honey syrup or Bourbon Honey Liqueur, and sour mix or fresh lemon juice. shake well and serve on the rocks with a slice of orange for garnish. I have a feeling whether it be national politics or barn politics, whiskey taken liberally with a good sense of humor may be the most sensible response when things just don't make sense

May 8, 2016

The Daily Bailey

"Of course, it's good to be here; at my age it's good to be anywhere." ~George Burns

Life is good today. I am 26 years old today! I hear we are celebrating with carrot cake on Monday when Mom gets back and I'm looking forward to that and a good ear scratching. She's been looking to find me a younger brother, although I've assured her, I'm happiest as an only child. She says don't be such a goose about it -no horse could ever replace me - but unless we find some Elven magic to restore my youth, something has to be found to pack her around the cross-country course for a few more years. Mom says trying to figure out if a horse is a good fit from a sale ad is like online dating - maybe worse. You agree to meet expecting a charming and amiable gentleman, only to find he is shorter than he appeared in his pictures, a bit nappy on the ground, and isn't very good at making eye contact. In all fairness, she did point out the nappy behavior was no fault of his own. Horses, like men, can become habitually naughty if allowed to behave badly without timely correction. Also, like men, when passed from person to person, horses survive by closing off a part of their heart. This doesn't necessarily make them unsafe, just harder to love. Mom says it is like trying to decide if you should keep looking for Mr. Right or go with Mr. Here Right Now. She doesn't think her luck with applying that approach to horses will get her any better results than it did with men in her younger years, so she's holding out for now. And she has completely sworn off looking at sale ads from other states. By the time she pays airfare to try it, a vet to pronounce it suitable for what she needs, and a driver to transport it, they would have to practically donate the horse to her to make it affordable. It's no wonder they call it the sport of kings. As she's telling me all of this, she looks up and reminds God, surely, He can help with this? and could He please send her the right one even if it's a mule? I think she should be careful what she prays for as I've seen God's sense of humor but that's between her and God. I'll just wait and see how He shows up and enjoy the show. Until then, I plan to enjoy her undivided attention, and use my charming good looks to get all the carrots, cookies, and ear scratches I deserve.

June 7, 2016

The Daily Bailey

"You get out of the horse what you put in — the way you put it in." ~Ray Hunt

Life is good today. Mom's been coming out to keep me brushed and polished even though it is dreadfully hot, too hot for even the bareback pad. She says at our collective age we have no need to prove anything - the fact that we are both on the same side of the ground and vertical is enough, thank you. She's been coming out at sunset and bringing me some icy cold watermelon, which is easier on my old teeth than carrots anyway. What a treat! She fills me in on all the latest horse news while she brushes me, and she told me something that really touched my heart about a boy named Mason. Mason rides a rescue horse named Luna, adopted from the horse sanctuary where he and his Mom and Dad volunteer. Over the weekend, he and Luna did their first show, taking first place in gaited pleasure and flags, and second in barrels and poles. Not bad for their first ride out! What impressed me, though, was not his performance. It was what he said to his mother about how he did: " I'm just really proud of my horse...it was her first show, and she did awesome". Now that is one good horseman in the making, if you ask me. A horse will try their heart out for you if you build that trust - and that takes time and patience most people your age is not willing to put in. Luna showed you how that pays off and I hope you have many more adventures with her. If you ever bring that fancy trailer with the living quarters out here to California, stop by and say hello, I'd like to meet you. Don't forget the carrots, partner.

July 1, 2016

The Daily Bailey

“It doesn't matter where you're from - or how you feel... There's always peace in a strong cup of coffee.” ~Gabriel Bá

Life is good today. Carried Mom around the outdoor as the sun went down - she says you know you've got a great horse when you can ride bareback on the buckle with a cup of coffee in one hand and the reins in the other. The mercury is slowly going down past the mark for Kuwait and is now nearing the mark that stands for the Equator, maybe by Sunday we'll hit the mark where humans and horses can be outdoors without danger of spontaneous combustion. The heat makes everyone irritable and sluggish. We were glad for the little breeze as we walked around the outside of the round pen, carrying the sounds from the pastures and barns around us. We fit each other like two worn old shoes these days, and I am grateful she didn't give up no matter how hard it was to ride me in the beginning. I am not the easiest horse to put together, and I admit I was a bit of a poop at times. It's the history between then and now that makes the now so much sweeter - for us both.

Her next horse will pick up where we left off - there will be lessons and flatwork and goals to work toward. Our only goal is to enjoy what time we have together and appreciate how very far we've come. She tells me what a grand horse I am as she brushes me and tucks me in with our favorite ritual: Kiss me you fool! she demands, and I brush my nose against her face in exchange for a carrot, or three. Now she has a mustache from the crumbs of grain in my bucket, but still pronounces mine the best lips she's ever kissed (and I hear she's kissed enough to know) before she turns to leave. Does it get any better than this?

July 9, 2016

The Daily Bailey

"We never know how God will answer our prayers, but we can expect He will involve us in the plans for His answer." ~ Corrie ten Boom

Life is good today. Mom made me laugh so hard today carrots almost came out my nose. She had a lesson on a horse named Simon yesterday - and she was so excited to talk about it that for a moment, I was jealous. Until she told me Simon was the equestrian equivalent of a drone -he's an equine simulator! I had visions of the mechanical bull, but she says he looks more like a Friesian, which is fine, as she is working on her position and seat for dressage. Simon is billed as the perfect schoolmaster - and indeed he is - he will never buck, bolt, or rear and his response to properly applied aids is always impeccable. Taking those factors out of the equation allowed her to focus on her own motor skills without the need to react to the unpredictability of us live models. She discovered that less really is more, one can open their hip angle within leaning backward or taking off the thigh (though not easily) and that holding your core does not require clenching of either the upper or lower abdominal muscles. She had no idea how instinctively and how often she clenched her glutes, which she suspects is the reason horses feel like lightning bolts are coming out of her backside. (This I'm sure will please Heather) And oh by the way, she is way out of shape. She is still praying to be sent the right horse, but she laughs when she says maybe this is the best right horse for now. Mandie and Kate will be happy to know that yoga classes were also recommended to improve flexibility. (Mom rolls her eyes at this one - yoga has never been on her bucket list but if it helps her ride better, she's resigned to including it) All in all, an unexpected but quite practical solution to the no horse problem. And speaking of answered prayers, I should thank Sally for helping Heather with Rather Swell when he is Rather Not - I heard he was a bit of a pill last show. Her insight into the kind of rider he needs for each phase was just what my first girl needed to hear. I will always love Miss Heather, so thank you Sally for helping her along. Mom says God tells us we have not, because we ask not - so she says there's no harm in asking, just don't be too surprised at how it shows up.

August 2, 2016

The Daily Bailey

"When we give cheerfully and accept gratefully, everyone is blessed." ~ Maya Angelou

Life is good today. After giving everyone a good scare last week by being found down in the pasture, I am happy to say I am almost back to my usual old self. The heat was just too much for this old boy, but thankfully Adriana saw me lying there and groaning so I wasn't there for long. Cheryl got the UC Davis Field service out, who tanked me up with several liters of fluid, and called Beth who arrived with her truck and trailer, just in case I needed to go in to the University. Dakota the horse kept watch over me, much like Beckett did when I was so very sick with laminitis years ago, until he saw I was up, on my feet and able to eat and drink again. Dakota the horse lives in the stall next to me, and we have become great friends since he's been there. Dakota, with his big ears, giant head and gentle nature, reminds me of my dear old Beckett, who I miss dearly. We even nap together, with our heads touching opposite sides of the same stall wall, like I used to with Beckett. Horses long for friendship much as humans do, and find it comforting knowing one is standing watch when they are not well. Mom learned a hard lesson about not remembering to keep her cell phone handy and charged - nobody could reach her and by the time they did, I was nearly back to normal. She couldn't apologize enough to me for not being there when I needed her. I don't think she'll soon forget that one. Her friend Laura even came out to check on me, because she was so worried when they had not been able to get ahold of Mom. Now that's a blessing - when you have a friend who doesn't even own a horse, but, knowing how dear your horse is to you, not only checks on him, she even comforts him for you! After all the excitement, I'm happy to say I'm none the worse for wear, although Mom was a little rattled. I have an extra fan on my stall now, thanks to Cheryl, who along with Trish, manages my pasture time like clockwork. Mom and I are ever so grateful for the love and concern our friends and our barn family show us - and we thank you!

August 5, 2016

The Daily Bailey

"Obsessing about your health doesn't actually make you healthier. The fact of the matter is... our bodies are decaying at every moment, regardless of what we do. Living is bad for your health...You can either embrace the dirt and the germs as part of the risky joy of living ... or you can spend lots of mental real estate obsessing over whether you touched a few extra microbes..." ~ Zack

Love Life is good today. Mom thinks she has finally figured out how I can help her earn enough money to retire early. Apparently, the New England Journal of Medicine has discovered what most of us who grew up in the country already knew - children raised on a farm are healthier and have less asthma. But wait, there's more. The findings of this ground-breaking study were so powerful, researchers are wondering if a spray made from barnyard dust could be made and given to children who are not lucky enough to be raised on a farm. Now that beats all. Wait 'til Dr. Mendoza hears this one. They put what in a metered dose inhaler? Yup. Barn dust. Mom says the drug companies will find a way to patent it, which means it will be years before it becomes available generic, which means it won't be on our formulary no matter how well it works. So, we are going to advertise me as a cost-effective, non-steroidal and homeopathic remedy which provides significant protection from asthma. If Dulera can get a piece of the market simply by using the word significant, Mom's convinced it will work for us. For a flat rate, she will offer stall-cleaning, grooming, or barn chore sessions which initially start with a 2-hour visit. Boosters can be provided weekly for six months, and then monthly thereafter for three to five years. A commercial, like the one for Gardasil, will make parents feel like child-killers for failing to provide something they were told could prevent even one case of dreadful disease. Fear can be a powerful economic motivator, and why let the pharmaceutical companies be the only one to tap that market. She might even try to convince Blue Cross that buying her a barn and filling it with horses, a cow or two, and a few chickens would be cheaper than paying for inhalers and emergency room visits.

After all, it's evidence-based medicine, is it not? The study has better data than those published for some of the inhalers she's encouraged to prescribe, as far as she's concerned. They can call it the Barnyards for Breath Project and put me in one of those trendy commercials with the voice of the woman from the West Wing. Mom says this just might be the biggest thing since penicillin, and when she stops laughing about all the potential applications, she may get around to developing our business plan. I say bring on the children and let them revel in the dusty glory of a barn filled with hay, horses, barn cats, barn dogs and a cow or two. Life is too short NOT to live like you were born in a barn!

September 6, 2016

The Daily Bailey

"To give real service, you must add something which cannot be bought or measured with money, and that is sincerity and integrity." ~ Douglas Adams

Life is good today. Mom says she needs to spend more time here with me than ever before because she is sure now the health care system has gone to hell in a handbasket and somehow, she has to last a couple more years to get that pension. She made me laugh so hard I almost spit hay out my nose - she told me about an email she got at work and when I heard how she responded; I couldn't help myself. Age is not mellowing this woman at all, it seems! Someone had the poor taste to invite her to participate in a conference about Mindfulness in Practice - supposedly to help other employees learn this as a means of improving employee engagement, productivity, health and well-being in the workplace. The group extending the invitation was called the Human Capital Institute, and they proclaimed their mission as finding the intersection of business, mindfulness and well-being. Well, her hair was on fire, I tell you, because first of all, since when do human beings get labeled as 'capital', and second there is no such thing as an intersection of business and mindfulness and well-being. Business is designed to generate and retain revenue and will resist any practice that does not fall in line with that goal. Case in point: line of people waiting to register for appointments, one reception clerk for six departments. Line winds down the hall and nearly to the elevators, including old and frail folks in wheelchairs or with walkers and oxygen. The right thing to do would be to ensure there is a second receptionist to handle the high-volume registration times. What happened? someone from administration came out to hand out teddy bears, to people who had waited in line more than 30 minutes to register for their appointments. A teddy bear. Mom rolled her eyes and said Bailey, I'm sorry but this new fascination with mindfulness in practice is like singing lambs who are going to slaughter a lullaby - they might feel warm cozy on the way, but eventually, they'll end up lamb chops.

She says if businesses really want to put their money where their mouth is, make the decisions that reflect sincerity and integrity of practice. Forget all this psychobabble about performance and quality metrics and just do the right God damn thing for Christ's sake. Ohh, she was hot, that's for sure - nearly curried a bald spot on my left flank before she wound herself down! Barn chores have a way of settling you, however. Later, as she put me to bed and scratched my ears (oh how I enjoy that) she thanked me for listening and told me how the only things that she knows to be real and true are God and horses. And she thanked me for reminding me of the goodness in both. I don't know how I'd last in her world - horses don't lie, they only are what they are in the moment. But I nudged her shoulder and reminded her that whenever she needs me, I'm right here at the intersection of sincerity and integrity. And like Motel Six, I'll leave the light on for her.

October 21, 2016

The Daily Bailey

"Stardom isn't a profession; it's an accident." ~Lauren Bacall

Life is good today. I'm feeling my age this time of year, and while I'm not feeling much like being ridden, I am always up for a good grooming, some ear rubs and a carrot or three. Mom says I shouldn't worry, my only job these days is to be the object of her affections and a good listener, which is fair exchange for carrots and ear scratches. Now if you know my Mom, you never know what might come out of that mouth so agreeing to listen may be more than you bargained for. Bailey, she said, you will never believe what I did today - Dakota and I got a part in an episode of a true crime series for tv! I got to dress up like a cop: gun belt, (complete with air pistol) badge, and walkie talkie. Dakota was a K9! He got to sniff out evidence that helped catch the killers! Well actually, it was sausage, because he isn't really a K9 but all's fair in the name of good footage when it comes to making movies. The crazy thing is, it was two chance meetings that brought it all about. Whether you call it synchronicity or serendipity, or fate, Mom says it doesn't matter. It was a surprise and a delight, and she had the most fun she's ever had, at least with all her clothes on. I wonder if they would ever need a bay thoroughbred gelding. I fancy myself as the Cary Grant type, to be honest. I think the camera would love me. Don't you?

October 30, 2016

The Daily Bailey

"Odd how much it hurts when a friend moves away leaving only silence." ~ Pam Brown

Life is good today. The big old thoroughbred who lived in the stall next to me left a few days ago, and hasn't returned, so I'm a bit unraveled by the empty stall, and find myself a bit melancholy without his company. I've grown quite fond of this fellow - he's been the first chap to make me laugh since my dear friend Beckett passed years ago - oh how I miss my old friend "Bucket"! Mom explained that my stablemate hasn't passed, like Bucket, his owner simply moved him to another barn. She could see how worried I looked, and allowed me walk around in his empty stall, now stripped and bare to the stall mats. I was both sad and relieved there was still the smell of him especially along the common wall between our stalls. Some people think horses aren't sentient beings; I've even heard that some believe our brains are only as big as walnuts. If they thought for a moment about how big our hearts are, they might realize the capacity we have to feel. They also forget that despite our tolerance for domestication, we remain instinctual herd animals by nature. Our herd in captivity becomes the horses confined around us, and our social interactions here are no less important in shaping the quality of our daily life. The most loving human and the best of care does not alter the fact that horses need the company of other horses, and to behave like horses to the extent they can. Heather says I'll be fine in a day or so, and I suspect she's right. Bel is still here right across the barn aisle, although like most mares she runs hot and cold. Still, she's been part of my 'herd' for years now - and occasionally tolerates my attention. Odin is still here, but he's up for sale, so no use getting attached to him, and he's a bit mouthy for my taste. The rest are mares, and all I will say about that is you can always tell a mare, but you can't tell her much. Cassie squeals like a banshee, and Lacey and Spring would put the fear of God into you with their mare stare. What's a fellow to do? Mom made me laugh - she said if she could bribe Georgina to certify me as a service animal, she'd put me in the backyard with a Dutch door so I could pop my head into the kitchen whenever I wanted company. Someday she'd like a place where I can wander safely about at will, like old Walker out at Feather Ridge - that suits me perfectly. In the meantime, I shall consider myself fortunate that the farewells in my life have been painful but few. Unlike some horses, passed on or sold from one owner to the next, I've belonged to Heather and Mom for most of my 26 years in this life- and they couldn't love me more. Heather still visits me whenever she can, which means the world to me. Horses remember and miss the humans who have loved them too! Being creatures who are very much in the moment, thankfully we don't dwell on these partings - especially when we have humans who love us through them. So, to my friend Dakota the horse, be well my good friend! I will miss your tomfoolery and silliness. Do take care, old chap! May your carrots be plenty, your farewells few, and until we meet again, happy trails from your old friend Bailey.

November 12, 2016

The Daily Bailey

"How is it that animals understand things I do not know ...perhaps there is a language ...not made up of words, and everything in the world understands it. Perhaps there is a soul hidden in everything, and it can always speak, without making a sound, to another soul." ~ Frances Hodgson Burnett

Life is good today. Mom says Danny Boy came home from the hospital and is healing nicely after an infection threatened the corrective surgery done on his legs. Danny Boy is a young Tennessee Walking horse who came to the horse rescue with severe leg deformities from birth defects, which the owners were told would correct themselves over time. This of course did not happen, and Danny Boy was sold to another family using the same story. By the time he reached Forget Me Not Horse Rescue in Missouri, his legs were so deformed it was a miracle he could walk at all, but this didn't stop Danny. He is as sweet and loving a horse as you'll ever meet - and a prankster from what I hear, as well. Some horses just speak to the souls of those around them in ways that are nothing less than endearing. There is nobody at the rescue who doesn't just love being around him - but the stark reality is that love doesn't pay the bills. In a business dependent upon donations, hard choices have sometimes got to be made. You can either feed horses or fix horses but there are days you can't do both. Now some would argue the value of choosing to make Danny's life more comfortable because in truth, even after the surgery, he will never be able to be ridden. But Mom says the concept of usefulness only matters if you define value by the concept of use. Thankfully many other people felt that way, too. - donations came that allowed horses to be both fed and fixed this time. We are glad to have you back in the sanctuary, Danny Boy! Try not to be too upset about the stall rest thing, it will be over before you know it, and you will be back to stealing carrots and hearts in no time.

December 4, 2016

The Daily Bailey 'I believe in kindness. Also, in mischief." ~ Mary Oliver

Life is good today. I managed to pull an entire bag of those tasty German horse cookies through the stall bars and had eaten a goodly portion of them before Mom figured out what I'd done. Mom had stuffed them into the blanket bar, thinking they were well beyond my reach; as soon as she turned away to put the grooming tote back, I proved her wrong. She tried to scold me but gave up because she was laughing too hard.

Once I pulled her saddle pad and her jacket right off the saddle rack in front of my stall and tossed it in the shavings. I couldn't keep a straight face as she wandered around wondering how on earth, they could disappear the moment her back was turned. My favorite tomfoolery is getting ahold of the Christmas stockings - and swinging them around like a stripper's panties until the candy canes and other goodies fall out - so I can pick the choicest morsels. If you've never seen a horse with a Christmas stocking dangling from his mouth and twirling it around, peppermints and candy canes flying everywhere, you don't know what you've been missing! Mom says it's a good thing I'm cute otherwise I'd be in a lot more trouble. She sat on a bucket in my stall for a good long while today while I finished my hay, because she misses me. She says I have a new sister, and that she's little and Welsh, whatever that means. She lives at another barn, so now Mom has two of us to take care of. I think I might like to meet her one day - I miss my friend Dakota who moved away last month. The new little Haflinger who moved in hasn't warmed up to me yet, and I could use another friend. Mom says her name is Ellie, and she is just as mischievous as I am - but like me, her saving grace is that she's as kind as she is naughty. I'm ever so glad if I must have a sister, at least she's a kind soul. Well little Miss Ellie, I look forward to meeting you one day and to some high - spirited shenanigans!

December 29, 2016

The Daily Bailey

"The greatest cruelty of age is that you only age on the outside." ~ Mary K. Moore

Life is good today. I got the best Christmas present of all this year - a visit from someone I love dearly. I didn't recognize her when she first opened the door to my stall - I knew the voice, but the face belonged to a beautiful young woman I couldn't seem to place. My vision isn't what it used to be; you know. It was only as she came closer that I realized who it was - my own dear Heather. How I have missed her! I could tell she was shocked by how much I've aged these past few years - my body hangs loose on my bones without the muscle I used to have, and the sway in my back is now unmistakable. I was sad to see tears in her eyes. I didn't want her to feel sorry for me, remembering me as an old and shuffling horse. Inside this old body, I'm still the quick, brave-hearted thoroughbred she trusted to carry her over and through any obstacle on that cross-country course. We never had a refusal - I'd give my life for that girl. Mom said watching those you love grow old sometimes feels like you are losing them by degrees. You grieve a hundred little losses before you mourn the loss of their actual physical presence. She also says it's just as hard for the one who is aging. She asks herself at least seven times a day who that woman in the mirror is, because SHE could not possibly be that old. In her heart, she says she never feels the age her driver's license insists she is. I was quick to remind her at times, she doesn't act the age her driver's license says she is, either. But truth be told, neither do I. I can still buck and carry on out in the field on a good day - and more than once Cheryl has had to come and catch me because I won't let myself be caught by anyone else. I guess it's a good thing Mom and I are growing old together - at least we have something in common. Horses stay young in their hearts too, if they are well-loved and cared for, which thankfully I am. Look past the earthly body I am in and you will still see the spirit of that thoroughbred heart, Heather. Keep visiting me as often as you can; whisper again to me the stories of our adventures and rub my ears until I doze off against your shoulder. Keep me young in your heart.

February 26, 2017

The Daily Bailey

"There comes a time when you realize turning the page is the best feeling in the world, because there is so much more to the book than the page you were stuck on." ~ Zayn Malik.

Life is good today. Mom came by to see me today and while she was currying out my winter coat (which is falling out by the handfuls) she told me we were moving! I am going to be in the same barn as Ellie, my new sister - and Mom says by the looks of my coat I'm taking half the footing of the indoor arena with me. She says I will have a nice long paddock attached to my stall so I can go outdoors and stretch my legs if I want to, or just enjoy the sun. She thinks I'll be next to a horse named Wensleydale, and across the aisle from Ellie. That way, Mom gets to see both of us every day. If I'm polite to Ellie, we might even get to be turned out together - oh how I miss the days when I was turned out with my dear friend Beckett! Horses are not solitary by nature, you know; we do best in the company of other horses. Andy and Coquetta are already there - I remember them! and Chris is there too! How I miss that woman. Mom says I'm too young at heart to stand in the corner of my stall and nap all day; being in a busy barn will be good for me. There will be lots of people I can nicker to as they pass by my stall, and my good looks and charming ways will earn me more than a few treats. Frankly, that sounds wonderful. I wasn't ready to be old yet anyway!

April 15, 2017

The Daily Bailey

" There may be times when we are powerless to prevent injustice, but there must never be a time when we fail to protest." ~ Elie Wiesel

Life is good today. Wensleydale returned home earlier this month, and in his place is a gigantic but ever so pleasant chap they call Hawk. Hawk is so tall he doesn't even have to stretch his neck to hang his head over top of the stall door - and quick to learn that eye contact with Mom = carrots. He's far more friendly than the horse on the other side of me - who is quite nappy - I don't know what his issue is but he doesn't care for anybody, and therefore gets no carrots. I've even met a couple of horses from the Czech Republic, who seem to spend most of their time lying on their side sleeping. Mom assures me this is no reflection upon the Czechs, who in general are known to have a good work ethic. I am glad to be in the same barn as Her Highness, oh, so sorry - I meant to say the little Highland mare. I like having a big paddock to roam about, and I like being with Chris and Tara and Aimee again, watching all the activity makes me happy. Mom usually takes us both out to graze in-hand while the grass is still green and tasty, so she can talk to us about the things that trouble her about people, the world, and especially the state of health care these days. She's in hot water again for speaking her mind, which if you know my Mom, should come as no surprise - she's never been one to keep quiet about dishonesty or injustice - especially when the welfare of others is at stake. Unfortunately, this makes her a lightning rod in the inevitable storm of controversy which follows. Mom says a man named Bertrand Russell once said that men fear thought like they fear nothing else on earth - because thought that does not bend to the will of established institutions and questions authority is considered subversive and revolutionary. Thought, he said, looks into the great pit of hell, and is not afraid. Well, I told her, through a mouthful of rye grass, it's a good thing you are made of steel, I've heard only the best lightning rods are. She laughed when she heard this, and we both knew that it was the truth - some people are just made that way because they have to be. Someone has to be strong enough to pick up the flashlight, and not be afraid to shine the bright light of controversy into things which prefer the dark. The brighter the mind, the brighter the flashlight. Her comfort lies in the fact that authority's only power is in the control of actions; it cannot control thought. and will never compel the mind to believe the power to exercise absolute control is leadership. Horses have known this principle since man first climbed upon our back; true horsemanship understands and respects it. Ellie then piped in to say that nobody likes an alpha mare until she saves the herd, so for the love of God, what did she expect?

Mom laughed even harder at that, and told her she sounds just like Heather, and she is absolutely right. If only Mom could pin her ears flat back and bare her teeth like a mare and give them the mare stare! In the meantime, she's grateful for the wisdom we give her, because it keeps her grounded in all she believes to be right and true.

May 10, 2017

The Daily Bailey

"A birth-date is a reminder to celebrate the life as well as to update the life." ~ Amit Kalantri

Life is good today. I am celebrating many years of life today - I say many because neither Mom nor I can remember if I am 24 or 26 years old. My chart at UC says I was born in 1993, but Mom's pretty sure my USEA registration says 1991. Only Heather remembers the exact day, of which she reminds Mom yearly. Mom says when you get old enough, making room for new data means something gets erased from the hard drive; what year or day isn't so important as the celebration of another year of life. Like her Aunt Marge says, 'Every day I'm above ground is a good day at my age'. Mom made me a carrot cake to share with everyone at the barn and brought me some shredded carrots to eat. My teeth are pretty worn these days - but not my spirit. Tara has a pretty new mare she hasn't named yet that I fancy, who whinnied to me a few days ago passing by. Even in my golden years, I can still make the fillies call. There's more gray in my forelock this year, which Mom says makes me look ever so handsome. I'm sure most of them were caused by her, and she agrees but thanks me for my tolerance and patience while I acquired them. I am so excited about my first girl Heather coming to visit this weekend! I haven't seen her since Christmas and I so enjoy her ear scratches. I am thankful for the opportunity to share my stories in the Daily Bailey, I feel as if I've come to know so many of you from stories shared by Mom. Please come meet me one day if you haven't already. Today would be a good day, as there's cake! But come any day and look for the dashing bay gelding with the white snip on the left side of the training barn. I'll nicker to you, so you know who I am. Yes, it is a very, very good life

June 15,2017

The Daily Bailey

" Sometimes the road of life takes an unexpected turn, and you have no choice but to follow it to end up in the place you are supposed to be." ~Khusbu Shaw

Life is good today. Mom had been walking me around the property after she rides Ellie most days, and she lets me decide if I want to graze, or take turns rolling in every one of the turnouts if I want to. She says at my age I get to do pretty much whatever makes me happy and she's glad to be a part of it. Sometimes we talk, sometimes she just leans against me and watches me graze. Lately she's talked about how very happy she is for her friends Jen and Brian - they've moved onto twenty- two-acre farm -and now have all their horses with them. Jen loves looking right out the window and seeing them; she's found farm life to be demanding but more rewarding than she ever imagined. Mom laughs - several months ago, a farm wasn't even on the radar - but life is like that sometimes. A series of events that fall like dominoes leading you to what you think is a dead end, only to find it's a door to blessings and contentment beyond measure. Their horses are rescues from a nearby sanctuary where the whole family volunteers. They like their new pastures and seem to be settling in well. Jen would like some chickens but she's not sure Bella the German Shepherd wouldn't want them even more, so they're holding off on more livestock for now. Mom's decided she may just take a road trip out to Missouri and teach Jen how to put up some of the produce growing in their garden; maybe show her how to make jam with whatever fruit they've got growing. Passing on those proper farm girl skills that country folk know. In a world that feels like it's going straight to hell in a handbasket, Mom says skills like this may be all that stands between us and starvation one day. Always good to be prepared. She says if I'd learn to talk like Mr. Ed maybe we'd be able to afford our own little piece of farmland, and she'll put a Dutch door on the back of the house so I can poke my head in whenever I feel so inclined. I just laughed.

But the more I thought about it, I began to think that was a pretty grand idea. I don't know about the talking part yet. She does enough talking for the two of us and then some. But if we ever do get some land, I hope she plants rows and rows of carrots. And alfalfa. I hear it's good for the soil.

July 13, 2017

The Daily Bailey

"Endurance is not just the ability to bear a hard thing, but to turn it into glory." ~ Wm. Barclay

Life is good today. Mom showed up today using the funniest sticks I've ever seen to help her walk and a big black metal thing on one leg that smells like hospital. I was so glad to see her! I'm not sure what happened to her leg, but it certainly didn't interfere with her dragging a grain bucket along behind her to bring me some stable mix - although she was swearing by those last few steps - something about sweating like a whore in church. Not that I know what a whore is but apparently, they aren't very comfortable in church. The walking sticks make her look funny and I don't like the smell of that thing on her leg, but it was ever so nice to have her sit on the feeder in my stall and give me an ear scratch. She can lean on me to scratch my withers, too. She says she'll be off work for a few months until she can put weight on her leg again, but she won't be idle. She's got that collection of horse stories she wants to get edited and published before Christmas and finish the book about how to be a barn mother for eventers. I think she should collect my Dailey Baileys and put them in a book, too. It would make a great stocking stuffer! I also think she should make more of those fancy hats. I like to pull them off her head and chew on the flowers, but someone might fancy one enough to buy it. Beats renting me and the pony out for birthday parties, if you ask me. Chris has some sit-down tasks she can complete, too. Mom is not one to sit idle, I can tell you that. Whatever happened to her leg hasn't broken her spirit and hasn't bruised her faith so I'm looking forward to how she'll use this - I certainly hope it gets me a book deal and an interview with Oprah. I'm sure she'd find me charming!

July 19, 2017

The Daily Bailey "The greatest cruelty is our casual blindness to the despair of others." ~ J. Michael Straczynski

Life is good today. The barn is being overtaken by chickens! Some say they help keep down the fly population, I personally prefer fly strips, as they don't nest in my feeder or poop all over the blanket bars, but to each his own, I suppose. Under the current free-range policy, I certainly hope there are no plans to acquire pigs. Even I have my limits. Mom says she's just about hit her limit with this broken leg business. Do you have any idea, she asked, how difficult it is to navigate with a walker or crutches in a world built for able-bodied people? So that's what they call those funny sticks she was using - crutches. Today she showed up pushing something with a basket with jump flags on either side, and a stuffed pony head on the front. I didn't mind it, but Lexington wheeled around and ran into his paddock as if the devil himself was perched on it. He refused to come into his stall, snorting, all puffed up out in the paddock, even after Mom dragged the whole contraption into my stall. Silly goose, had he known that basket was full of carrots, he might have found some courage. Mom sat on the edge of my feeder and talked to me while I ate my stable mix; my teeth are too old and worn down to do much justice to hay, so I like my bucket of softer pelleted forage. She said with all the progress we've made toward ensuring access to places for disabled people, she was astonished to realize that unless you were confined to a wheelchair, most of the able world remained inaccessible, or accessible with great difficulty if you had to use crutches or a walker instead. Take sidewalks, for example. The grooves for drainage that wheelchairs roll over - they catch the tips of crutches or the wheels of a walker, which if not for her cat-like reflexes, would have pitched her forward flat on her face. And those yellow ramps? Why are they textured like legos? Again, neither crutch nor walker friendly. One would think a medical center would be designed for disabled people to navigate easily. Wrong again. Only one handicapped entrance at each end of the main buildings. In between, yards and yards of grooved walkways and then occasional yellow lego ramp. Entirely possible you might require trips between two buildings and three departments for one doctor's visit! I told her she should just snag the mini pony from the front paddock and make it pull her in a cart. She laughed and said she'll be in enough trouble when she goes back for her recheck and the trauma surgeon sees hay, shavings, and maybe even bits of manure on the wheels of her walker. Whoever oversees deciding what gets built for the differently able has clearly never realized not everyone with limited mobility needs a wheelchair. I told her maybe the wheelchair people just have a more powerful lobby. Well that just set her hair on fire- now she's talking about decorating walkers and storming the state capital with as many people as she can muster using walkers, crutches, and canes. Lord have mercy.

August 29, 2017

The Daily Bailey

"Everyone who is born holds dual citizenship, in the kingdom of the well and in the kingdom of the sick. Although we all prefer to use the good passport, sooner or later each of us is obliged, at least for a spell, to identify ourselves as citizens of that other place." ~ Susan Sontag

Life is good today. There is a bit of a breeze which is making this unsufferable heat more bearable, and I'm relieved to finally see Mom again. She didn't come visit us for three entire weeks! This is so unlike her - and to tell the truth I was quite worried, but then she explained that she had been dreadfully ill. In fact, she said, if not for her roommate, she might have ended up as nothing more than a strange smell on the second floor. Everyone was convinced it was something she caught from the new little puppy, but it turned out to be a serious infection from some contaminated chicken she had handled. I can't even pronounce the name of the bacteria she said it was. She says if she never sees raw chicken again, she'll not be sorry. She doesn't really care to see live chickens either, running amuck as they are amongst the stalls, but that's another story. Even after two trips to the Emergency Department and nearly three days in the hospital, it took two more weeks to feel like she was going to stay among the living. In the meantime, Orthopedics was amazed to find her fracture almost completely healed - which she is convinced is a combination of good old- fashioned Baptist prayer warriors, (thank you Auntie Penny) and bone glue - otherwise known as calcium with vitamin D3. Being too sick and too weak to move around much probably didn't hurt, either. People like her don't slow down unless a train hits them, and even then, they're insisting there are only minor wounds and continue to press on. Say what you will, being flattened probably had some value in preventing her from being as active as she would have liked. Rest is a four- letter word for her. I am ever so glad to have her back. I got a good currying and some wither scratches today - reminded me so of my dear friend Beckett, who would groom me with his teeth like that. How I miss Beckett! Before she left, Mom took off my fly mask so she could see my handsome face, and, sitting on the edge of my corner feeder, rubbed my ears and talked to me 'til I nearly fell asleep. It's good to have her back.

September 16, 2017

The Daily Bailey "Zombies: It's all fun and games until someone gets bit." ~ anon.

Life is good today, but something very strange is going on around here. There is something that is just not right with a lot of the chickens. Yes, chickens. I know one would not expect flocks of chickens in a boarding stable but there are a lot of things one does not expect here yet endure as the price of doing business with a boarding stable. The chickens came sometime in late spring, right after the forty goats disappeared. The goats smelled a lot worse than the chickens, but I must say, at least they were cute. A few days ago, many of the chickens began to look unwell. I even overheard some of the boarders say they saw a lot of very unwell chickens lying about near the pen which was supposed to contain them. The sick chickens wander around in circles, bumping into walls, or fall forward on their chicken faces, followed by feeble attempts to right themselves. Some have deformed eyes. It's quite unsettling, I can tell you. Mom calls them zombie chickens. She says there really are such things as zombie chickens and if you don't believe it talk to some farmers in Petaluma where they have experienced it firsthand. Being the conspiracy theorist, she is, she can't help but wonder if it has something to do with biological warfare research. Chicken eggs are often used to grow viral cultures, you know. If that's the case, she thinks the Russians are probably involved as they've been tied to almost everything else going to hell these days. I bet she's been listening to George Nouri and that program called Coast to Coast again on late night radio. I stopped chewing my hay and looked her straight in the eye. Really? I said. She laughed and said she won't worry until she drives up and sees men in Tyvek suits and NIOSH95 respirators tenting the barns. Or, until she sees a chicken with blue eyes. Then she's breaking out the dragon glass. She's pretty sure she can find some on Amazon, they have almost anything else. She hopes something like that would be Prime eligible, so she can get it overnight. John Snow may know nothing, Bailey, but I am prepared! Where does she get these ideas? She just laughed and said it's more than likely some virus common to poultry which poses no threat to humans or horses, but unless one is tested, we won't know for sure. Apparently, the lab needs a fresh dead chicken, which seems like an oxymoron but that's what the man said. She is not likely to volunteer for that job. First of all, she's not going to follow a staggering chicken until it finally keels over. And if she did, and started to stuff said zombie chicken into a ziploc bag, what if it suddenly opened it's one good eye to look back at her? Oh HELL no. That task will have to be assigned to someone who is comfortable working with the undead. The whole incident has only deepened her distaste for poultry - whether it be running amuck in the barn, staggering about like a zombie, or naked and cold on a Styrofoam tray. She'll be glad when they are gone. Good Lord, I just had a thought. if they have to get rid of the chickens, and they can't have the goats, I hope dairy cows or pigs aren't next! I think Mom needs to get us our own place and the sooner the better.

October 18, 2017

The Daily Bailey "Finding an old friend is like finding a lost treasure." ~ Anthony Douglas Williams

Life is good today. I got to see my old friend Bel this past Sunday! Bel is a beautiful mare, and although she can be quite keen under saddle, she is fond of older men and likes to flirt with me. Well, who wouldn't? Our moms have been friends for years now, and for most of that time we've been stabled right across the barn aisle from one another. Our moms would let us play itchy withers every chance we got when nobody was looking, because management frowned on it. Itchy withers is when two horses scratch and groom each other's necks and backs (or in some cases, rumps) at the same time with their teeth, which act like giant backscratchers. It is great fun for the most part, until someone's knickers get in a twist because one gets a bit rough. That's when the squealing might begin and that's why management frowns on it - squeals can be followed by kicking and biting. Our moms know that as long as both horses remain respectful of one another, it is very comforting and in fact important for the horses to be able to do this. We are herd animals, and this kind of mutual grooming behavior is one way we create social bonds. In a boarding barn, your herd becomes the horses around you, or the horses that belong to the friends that surround your mom. Now that Bel and I live in different barns, I only see her if she comes for lessons, and I miss her. It's not that the horses here aren't friendly. Hawk is a good egg, and quite personable. My friends Coquetta and Andy are here -] I just miss my old friends. Old friends are the keepers of your history. They remember your best days, and suffer with your through your worst, holding both in their hearts. Beckett and Hi have already crossed over into the light, so Bel is the last one living of my herd from the past two barns. Like Beckett and Hi, we share a history. I remember when Val first brought her home off the track - she was a leggy three- year old and didn't know the first thing about eventing. She didn't know how to be anything but a racehorse! I became her four-legged babysitter, which was comical if you want to know the truth. My mom is probably one of the timidest riders ever when it comes to jumping - but she would pony on me alongside any horse because she knew she could trust me to be sensible. Even alongside a wild-eyed off the track thoroughbred mare who might not have all four feet on the ground at the same time. Sometimes blind faith and ignorance really are bliss. I remember when I gave Bel a lead into the water complex at Woodside - I'll never forget the look in her eyes - she was sure(as Val would say) that I'd lost my ever-loving mind stepping into that shiny wet ground that made strange splashing noises and gave way at our feet. I literally had to herd her through it before she understood it wasn't going to swallow her up.

The first time she went to the showgrounds in Fresno, Mom and I rode with her and Val around the track. Bel was so nervous - she kept leaning in towards me as thoroughbreds often do when they feel anxious and wouldn't settle at first. But Mom and I just rode alongside, reins nearly at the buckle until she finally sighed and settled into a walk. Mom and I were still competing then - Bel went with us for company and to learn the routine. And Lord could that mare whinny if I went anywhere out of sight! She would start calling for me the minute we left the mounting block and often didn't stop until we returned. I confess I often answered just as loudly, which unnerved Mom to no end. She said it felt like trying to balance on top of the washer during a spin cycle, with an unbalanced load. A horse's whole body vibrates when he neighs like that at the top of his lungs. We used to call Bel 'Green Bean' for the longest time, because an inexperienced horse is often called 'green'. Oh my. I really am getting old. Seems like so long ago. You're not a Green Bean any longer, Bel. I've watched you grow into a beautiful and brave mare. I'm glad you came to visit an old friend, and I'm so very thankful that like our moms, we have been part of each other's story.

January 16, 2018

The Daily Bailey "To care for those who once cared for us is the highest honor." ~ Tia Walker

Life is good today. Bill and Chris sent Mom a video of me wearing my new shoes which I am happy to say make me more comfortable (especially when I turn) than the bedroom slippers or the wooden clogs I had while my feet healed. Early in the summer I got laminitis again, and It's been a long road back. I'm happy that between my Mom, Chris, and a great farrier I am feeling younger than my almost 27 years, at least as far as my feet are concerned. Let me tell you, growing old is not for sissies. I am not oblivious to the fact that caring for an elderly horse takes no small effort, nor does it involve small sums of money. If it isn't my feet which need tending it's my teeth or my feed or my bedding which need adjusting, all of which come at a cost. Despite well-meaning advice to the contrary, Mom stubbornly refuses to send me packing to a less expensive retirement home - because she cannot bear the thought of not seeing me when she comes to the barn, and worries about who will care if I'm cold and need a blanket, or hungry and need more stable mix than hay, or pick the mud from my feet after standing in a soggy paddock all day. Instead, she says it's a good thing she likes peanut butter and jelly - there are times she eats a lot of it thanks to me - but then she hugs me and whispers in my ear she'd do it a thousand times over for what I've done for her and Heather and Tantzie and Georgina. She cannot find a way to justify not repaying me with the care she feels I have earned. She knows some people think she's crazy for feeling this way. I know she's crazy, but to be honest, as far as I'm concerned, I'm the better for it. I think about the horses who, after years of faithful service, end up spending their last days in a rescue or sanctuary - or worse. And then I look down at my Mom, who is now trying to take the mud out of my coat with a shedding blade; an endless task, as my coat is now so thick and shaggy Mom says I look more like a Yeti than a horse. But she does it anyway, because she hates to see me look neglected and as she calls it, like an old plow horse. What can I say? I turn toward her slightly, resting my head right on top of hers for a few moments and let out a big sigh. I am so grateful. She stops scraping and reaches up with one arm to hug my neck, and whispers 'you're welcome' into my ear.

February 8, 2018

The Daily Bailey "Tell the lizard to shut up." ~ Sam Godin

Life is good today. The days are becoming incrementally longer, and the February sun feels so good on these old bones. Mom went to a sports psychology workshop Saturday. After she fell off the pony last year, her broken leg healed but her broken confidence did not. It was what riders call a dirty stop - a sneaky and unpredictable thing horses do sometimes, even the best of them, and for Mom, it's been a hard road back. Even with Aimee and Chris to keep the pony going, Mom realized if she didn't figure this out soon, pony and the sport of eventing would soon be history. And then, in this workshop, she learned about the reptilian brain. Neuroscience has proven that when we are in a state of fear, we can't access all the parts of our brain - we can't really think because we only have access to a very primitive part of our brain called the reptilian brain. The reptilian brain can only help us eat, fight, run or breed. Some people call it the lizard brain. I think that's why Cheryl (who also attended the workshop) said operating with the reptilian brain while in the saddle was like letting a lizard drive the bus. This made Mom laugh. But the next day, when it was time to ride a combined test, that's exactly what happened - Mom let the lizard drive the bus. Because the lizard doesn't insist the pony be attentive or obedient, the dressage test was almost as ugly as Mom's state of mind afterward. Mom let the lizard convince her she couldn't do the jumping test- after all, they hadn't jumped more than a few poles since July, and if she couldn't get the pony decently around a dressage ring, there was no way in hell she was getting her around a course of jumps. When she passed my stall, she looked defeated. I was grateful to see Cheryl wander down the aisle to the cross-ties - I'm sure Mom was composing Ellie's sale ad as she removed the tack. Cheryl's quiet wisdom about horse behavior has helped many a rider see a problem as an opportunity, and in the end, thankfully this was no exception. I don't know exactly what was said, but before they left the barn for warm up, Mom was laughing, and had a resolve about her I haven't seen in a long time. I dare say the pony had no idea she was about to meet a whole new woman in that warmup. When the pony offered the same lazy canter, she had produced for the dressage test, Mom only had to use the crop twice, reminding the pony aloud had she paid attention the first time, the conversation would not require repeating. Apparently, this was all the incentive pony needed to recognize a lizard was no longer driving the bus; I understand they went on to jump a foot-perfect course without missing a stride. I hate to be snarky but it's about time that little tart of a pony got her comeuppance. Lord knows I've kept my opinions to myself about Miss Wonder Pony so far, but I do not appreciate my Mom being trifled with. The little Welsh princess is about to see a new world order. Good work Mom. It's great to see you back in the game.

April 26, 2018

The Daily Bailey " You only have one life. You may as well live it as a bad ass." ~ unknown

Life is good today. Mom gave me my first bath of the year, and then took me into the only grassy turnout. It would have been a lot nicer if the little paint who was in it first hadn't grazed it down to the nubbins, but I managed to find a longer tuft of grass here and there. My coat is so long Mom says I look like a Bakshir Curly. I don't know what they are, but apparently, they are very fuzzy like me. I'm getting clipped tomorrow and judging by how Ellie looked the first time Mom clipped her, I suppose it's a good thing I'm not showing anymore. Mom says she's taking the Ferrari pony to Woodland Stallion Station in a few weeks for a test drive in the Intro division. She thanked me for packing her around Intro and Beginner Novice all those years ago - if I hadn't taken such good care of her out on course, she probably wouldn't be competing right now. I love my first girl Heather, and I love my Mom. I'd jump the moon for either one of them. If it were up to me, I'd have carried them forever, but horses only have so many jumps in them and my competing years are done. It's the pony's turn now. Much as I make fun of her, calling her the Pony Brat and the little Welsh Diva, I secretly think Ellie has just as much heart for her job as I do. I think Mom is finally starting to believe that, too. They've had their ups and downs since the fall Mom took last summer and broke her leg, but I think they're sorting it all out. She wouldn't have fallen off today if she'd just stayed with the mare and let her jump the poles Mom forgot to steer her through. There went all the Land Safe stuff she was trying to keep in her head, and off the right shoulder she went like a Pop Tart out the toaster. Poppity ping as they say in Wales. There she was, cantering toward the vertical standing in one stirrup off the side, (where is the video camera when you can capture this kind of trick riding?) almost landing on her feet. But as she slowed, Ellie zigged and Mom zagged, landing on her butt - which I'm saying with all Christian love, has enough padding to absorb the impact. She forgot to let go of the reins 'til the last minute, so there went the roll cage she was supposed to make with her arms. Ellie headed straight for Chris, as any smart pony would do, because when you're dealing with amateurs, the trainer is the safest spot around. In true eventer fashion, Mom dusted the arena off her breeches, took the reins from Chris and got back in that saddle, this time, jumping a foot perfect round right out of stride. Even the hunters said it looked good! Mom said moments like that are priceless - she feels like such a badass. They remind her of who she really is - the kind of woman who looks a challenge in the eye, gives it a wink. I say go for it Mom. I think Ellie is just the pony who will help you do it, and I will be right here waiting to hear about each new adventure.

May 20, 2018

The Daily Bailey "I love the drama of a hat." ~ Phillip Bloch

Life is good today. Mom stopped by last evening and took me out to graze for a bit and told me all about the royal wedding. She just had to watch for the hats, you know, now that she's designing some of her own. She was quite pleased to see the Queen Mum favors beautiful flowers on her hats - in fact quite similar to the designs Mom favors. Wouldn't that be a lark, becoming milliner to the Queen? Although mom hardly thinks she shops on Etsy. She did not share the same gushing praise given by commentators for Camilla's choice. She said it looked like someone launched a giant Frisbee covered in ruffles, landing it on the side of her head. She admits she's never been much of a fan for Camilla's millinery choices, reminding me of the awful feathered model Camilla wore to her own wedding. In Mom's opinion (which I'm sure the royal court gives careful consideration) Camilla looked like a giant hedgehog. Fascinators seem more popular than ever - Mom likes these little headpieces - and thinks she needs to launch a line of these. She also noticed a trend she finds quite lovely - flowers in the hair on the underside of hats tilted carefully to one side -. Princess Kate wore this beautifully in pale pink. Oprah's hat was her favorite, and she was pleased to see so many vintage styles with netting and feathers. She thought Megan's mother was positively elegant in her 40's classic design. Mom says the wedding clearly showed that the difference in being dressed up and well-dressed lies in wearing a great hat, and I can't say she's wrong. I would find her beautiful in anything she wears, but I do like the flowered hats she wears - the blooms can be quite tasty. (I like to pull off her hat and carry it with my teeth - waving it up and down at her.) She says that's just the sort of behavior that prevents us from attending royal weddings, and she should scold me for it. She doesn't though, as it always makes her laugh. She calls me a scoundrel, but soon as she retrieves the hat from my mouth, she rubs my ears and tells me she wouldn't have it any other way. I suppose whether you wear them or prefer nibbling on them, hats do seem to be the perfect accessory. Life is short - wear the hat!

July 7, 2018

The Daily Bailey "Illusions are the truths we live by until we know better." ~ Nancy Gibbs

Life is good today. Mom told me if it weren't for me and Ellie, she'd probably be half mad by now as the whole world seems to be going insane. She used to think she earned an honest living in health care, but now, she's not so sure. She's never been one to tolerate duplicity, I can tell you that. She's often honest to a fault, which, while she admits makes her unpopular, allows her to sleep better at night. Medicine, she says, has become more about the marketing of what potential patients perceive as good medicine, than about the actual practice of good medicine. Apparently, the bean counters have discovered that when people feel emotionally connected to a business, they remain loyal and are willing to pay a premium price for their goods and services. Mom says this is called 'brand intimacy', and says it is part science, part technology, and part new religion. On the surface, it looks warm and fuzzy and touchy feely. The dark underbelly is another story. More money is being committed to making consumers believe they are having a wonderful health care experience than to the things that would provide a wonderful health care experience: more nurses to care for patients in the hospital, enough receptionists in the clinic so people on oxygen and in wheelchairs don't have to wait in long lines to register for appointments, enough pharmacy technicians to fill prescriptions so patients could get medications without waiting for 45 minutes. Mom calls it Facebook medicine, and it both annoys and saddens her that the experience of being cared for has turned into such a feeding frenzy for marketing sharks. Horses either like you or don't, based on how you treat them, and you can't fool them with cookies, or carrots, or sweet words. Mom says they need more horses in health care and less horse's asses - maybe things might get better. Then she laughed because she could just imagine what a horse would do in one of those staff meetings.... well, maybe not, I thought. She's not going to change how she takes care of people, that's for sure, it's such a part of her nature she couldn't if she wanted to. But I'm glad Ellie and I are here to keep it real and feed the part of her spirit that keeps good going.

July 30, 2018

The Daily Bailey "If we succeed in empowering girls, we will succeed in everything else". ~ Desmond Tutu

Life is good today. I had a nice long graze in the turnout down by the road, where a good deal of alfalfa grows in addition to some grass. Alfalfa is one of my favorite hays to munch on, but to get it green and fresh and straight from the ground - heaven. Mom brought out a little girl named Ellie, who has always wanted to ride horses. This happens to be one of Mom's favorite things to do - introducing children to horses. If it were up to her, it would be mandatory for every little girl to have a pony at least once in her life. She ticks off the names of every little girl she knew who grew up riding, starting with Heather, and reminds me that every one of them is in a pretty good place right now thanks to what horses taught them. Ellie looked to me to be about ten years old. Mom put her on Ellie the pony first, and they went around the indoor for a while. From what I hear, the child could be a natural - no fear, and they even trotted for as long as Mom could trot beside them on foot before running out of breath. After they put away the pony, Mom asked Ellie if she'd like to hop up on my back, and she'd walk her to the pasture with me. That was the quickest yes I've ever heard! Mom says all it takes is one touch for a girl to fall in love with horses, and I think for this little girl, she was probably right. She was quiet and gentle as she brushed me and spoke so kindly to me. Mom led me outside, and Ellie's auntie lifted her up onto my back. Mom stood there for a moment, trying to gauge how confident or fearful Ellie was before starting off down the drive, and laughed out loud when Ellie said, 'there's a lot of bones in his back'. Well, it's true! I'm not the most comfortable horse to sit bareback. Mom asked her how it felt to be up so high, and I heard the little girl say " I love it! It feels like I could climb mountains!". And Mom said yep, Ellie, that's how horses make you feel sometimes - like you can do anything. While we walked out to pasture, she told Ellie I made her feel like she could fly, and that I taught her to be brave, and trust me. She told her how we jumped logs and ditches and banks and galloped through water - and how I never once let her down - 'Oh I would love to see that! I would love to learn to do that!" Ellie reached down and hugged my neck. 'You're such a good boy, Bailey!" Mom hung out in the pasture with me for a while, as we watched Ellie and her aunt drive away. Mom thanked me for giving one more little girl a sparkle in her eye and kissed me on the nose. I thought about the little girls (and the little girls cleverly disguised as women) I have carried over the years - I have loved them all. I happy knowing that somewhere in all those rides, Mom says I taught them they are capable, gave them self-confidence, and a sense of accomplishment that went far beyond the barn. She thinks it's priceless. I'm too old now for another little girl, but I do hope Ellie gets the chance to chase her dream and finds a horse that makes her feel like she can climb mountains.

August 16, 2018

The Daily Bailey

"Healing invokes the power of compassion, both for yourself and for others...at this point, the healed may become a healer." ~ David Hawkins

Life is good today. I got out for a good stretch and some grazing in the alfalfa patch again, while Mom curried the salt, sweat and dust out of my coat left by the last heat wave. She says science is starting to recognize how therapeutic it is for humans to be around horses, proving what she's intuitively known for years now. Apparently horses and humans both have a field of electromagnetic energy that projects from their heart outward, like a big circle of energy surrounding them. A human's energy field might be 8-10 feet wide, but a horse's is FIVE times bigger! Can you imagine? Well I'm sure if they measured by breed, thoroughbreds (like me) would have the largest. We're known for our heart, you know. This energy field has healing properties, according to the research, by causing the release of endorphins, lowering blood pressure, and even directly affecting the human heart by lowering the heart rate, and a whole lot of other wonderful things. Some people call it fuzzy science (no pun intended) but Mom says it's only fuzzy because you can't measure academically something that is of the soul and the spirit. She thinks one day quantum physics will give us the scientific answers we seem to need to believe in the healing properties of energy, but until then she's content to believe without scientific proof. She says it must work this way with humans, too, because sometimes her own patients heal her in ways they could never know, and she would never have expected. While not always obvious in the moment, as she reflects upon a particular interaction, the insight often startles her, which I find quite curious. It doesn't surprise me in the least -horses intuitively know healing is an energy, and it goes in both directions if the heart is open. If Mom were a horse, she'd know this, but she's a human so her mind gets in the way sometimes. If her heart is open to anyone, her patients are at or near the top of that list, so it makes perfect sense to me that she would be just as often on the receiving end of that good energy as on the giving side! I don't know who her patients are, but I'm thankful for what they have given my Mom. Now if you all would be kind enough to come by with some nice fresh carrots, I'll share some of my wonderful horse energy, and I'll be happy to thank you in person!

September 9, 2018

The Daily Bailey " I hope I can be the autumn leaf, who looked at the sky and lived. And when it was time to leave, gracefully... knew life was a gift." ~ Dodinsky

Life is good today. A cooling trend is on the horizon, and my shaggy Cushing's coat will soon keep me warm on crisp fall nights. The days are getting shorter, and I see geese flying in formation south at almost every sunset now. It is the autumn of my life, too, I think, and that is hard for my Mom to bear. I have been awfully foot-sore even before my last shoeing, and the farrier has been clear that there is not much more he can do for these old feet of mine. It hurts to walk very far, and I have a hard time turning, so I don't really feel like coming out of my stall for a walk anymore -my feet hurt too much. I still like a good flake of alfalfa, and I love Mom's scritches on my withers - oh how it reminds me of my dear friend Beckett! I do enjoy hanging my head out the open door, and when Mom can coax me out for a little walk, I enjoy going up the aisle and visiting Misty and Red, who belong to Tara. I have had a crush on Misty, ever since she came to this barn. I hear my old girlfriend Coquetta will be moving back to this barn soon, too. I like to just hang out in front of their stalls and steal whatever scraps of hay are poking out of the feeders. (I have plenty of hay of my own, but someone else's always tastes sweeter, somehow.) Mom grooms me every night she is there, she says just because I'm old it's no excuse for looking unkempt. She scratches my ears, cups her fingers and scritches my withers like Beckett did, and scratches my neck. She sits on my feeder while she rubs my ears and talks to me about something called quality of life. She says she doesn't know what that means for me, and it makes her cry. I'm a horse, I don't understand that concept either, I just know I feel loved and even though my feet hurt so badly, I love seeing my Mom and eating and having her scratch my withers. Mom says I can go home anytime I want to, just let her know and she will help me pass over the bridge. She doesn't want to keep me here to be selfish. She says don't be upset if she cries, grief is just the price you pay for love. She will be at peace knowing I am not in pain anymore and warns me I had better come with Beckett when it's her turn to pass so she'll know she's going to heaven. I promise her that I will, but I'm not sure if I want to go home just yet. I hurt, yes. Can I walk comfortably? No. Not really. But I'm not lying down, there are still carrots to be had, alfalfa to eat, and my Mom's good company. Who's to say that's not a good quality of life for me? Mom says if I don't want to come out of my stall, I don't have to. She leaves the door open so I can hang my head out and - and if I'm happy eating and drinking and enjoying her company, that's ok with her. She'll wait to follow my lead. I do hope I get to see my Heather just one more time before I go home - I love my first girl! I would love to see Georgina and Tantzie and Lucca, too. I have had a good, good life, and I have been loved beyond measure, that I know for sure. Mom told me because of my Daily Baileys, there are people I haven't even met who know me and love me - can you imagine that? My time is coming, I know, I feel it. And when it does, I will let Mom know as best I can so she can be merciful and compassionate and pray me over into the light. Until then, I'm content to be loved, scratched, and fed.

September 25, 2018

The Daily Bailey "There is no real ending place. It is just the place where you stop the story." ~ Frank Herbert

Life is good today. I am finally home. Mom often told me that new beginnings are often disguised as painful endings, and I would have to admit that this was one of the most painful endings we have both endured. My feet and her heart were in the most excruciating pain one can imagine. Laminitis can be cruel and relentless. In some horses, it happens once and never recurs. In others, it becomes chronic, and may flare at any time even if every preventive measure is taken. The flares cause terrible pain that lasts for weeks, each time leaving the horse with a new level of chronic pain or disability. I was one of those horses. My mom gave me the best veterinary treatment money could buy, the best farriers she could find, and the most careful attention to what I ate and what I did - and still the laminitis came back. This was beginning to feel like one of the worst episodes I'd had in a long time. We could try powerful combinations of medications, which might, after weeks of suffering, give me some relief, but it would not prevent the laminitis from coming back. Mom has been very clear with me I can go home at any time - I just had to let her know when I was ready to be done. It broke my heart to tell her, but I finally felt that this time, I was done. I had no fight left in me. After 28 years, I wanted to go home. It broke her heart to hear, but she was wise and compassionate enough to listen. In the end, her love for me was greater than her wish to see me stay. She gave me the most loving transition a horse could hope for. The veterinary team from UC Davis sent the kindest and gentlest vets, who blocked my feet with Novocain so I couldn't feel the pain anymore. I got to walk out into the green grass with my Mom, and graze while we talked about going home and how much she loved me. We talked about all the memories we made, and how hard it is to say goodbye. She made me promise to let her know I was happy on the other side, and I made her promise to finish my book, and put my picture on the front cover. I told her my love for her was endless - I would be in her heart always and live on in the stories she would tell about our adventures. Il thanked her for the loving care she has given me in these many years of my life. Chris was there too, and I silently thanked her for teaching my Mom how I needed to be ridden, and for giving us the chance to ride those cross-country courses like champions. Mom held the phone to my ear so I could talk to my Heather, who is in Ireland with her Dad. She told me what a good boy I was, and how sorry she couldn't be there to give me a hug. She thanked me for all I had taught her and how I tried with all my heart for her when we competed. It was wonderful to hear her voice. I tried to tell her how sorry I was, and not to cry; that I needed to leave, that I knew how much she loved me, and that I would watch over her always. While I was happy eating grass, the vets gave me some medicine that made me very sleepy. I wanted to lie down for a bit, so they let me lie down. Mom held my head in her lap, and I fell asleep with her whispering in my ears how much she loved me, asking God to take me into his arms. When I woke up, I was as light as a feather. My feet didn't hurt anymore. I was walking on a rainbow toward a beautiful white light, when who do I see trotting toward me but my dear friend Beckett! He told me how happy he was to see me; he's missed me terribly and has been waiting for me here. I was so excited - I wanted to let Mom know how beautiful it is here, but she can't see me or hear me yet. Beckett says that's normal, her grief right now is too strong, but not to worry, in a while, I'll find ways to let her know. Her heart must heal first. He says he remembers his promise and now we can both be there to carry her over when it is her turn to pass. This is where my story stops on earth, but it doesn't end. The power in story, whether told by human or horse, is that it connects us. The story of one becomes the story of many, and the story of them becomes the story of us. Sometimes there is nothing as powerful or helpful to our souls as a story that reminds of the common truths and shared experiences of our hearts. I hope my story has brought encouragement to those who needed it, laughter at the absurdities of life, inspired action against injustice and indignity, and hope to those who sat in darkness with the reassurance that good will always prevail, and that life after all, really is good.

~ In loving memory of Bailey ~